QUILTED THROWS,
BAGS & ACCESSORIES

Quilted Throws, Bags & Accessories
Published in 2018 by Zakka Workshop, a division of World Book Media LLC
www.zakkaworkshop.com

134 Federal Street
Salem, MA 01970 USA
info@zakkaworkshop.com

KONO SANAE NO YOKU WAKARU PATCHWORK LESSON KAWAI MAINICHI NO QUILT
Copyright © 2014 Sanae Kono / NIHON VOGUE-SHA
Originally published in Japanese language by Nihon Vogue Co., LTD, Tokyo, Japan
English language rights, translation, and production by Zakka Workshop
Photographers: Toshikatsu Watanabe, Noriaki Moriya

Translation: Ai Toyoda Jirka
English Editors: Lindsay Fair and Kristyne Czepuryk

ISBN: 978-1-940552-33-0

Printed in China
10 9 8 7 6 5 4 3 2 1

QUILTED THROWS, BAGS & ACCESSORIES

28 Inspired Projects Made with Patchwork, Paper Piecing & Appliqué

Sanae Kono

This book is dedicated to quilters of all experience levels: beginners who have an interest in quilting but aren't sure if they're doing things right, lapsed quilters who find themselves returning to the craft after some time away, and even those veterans who are still eager to learn new designs and techniques.

I believe that the secret to making beautiful quilts lies in mastering the basics. Have you ever found yourself stuck in the middle of a project because your seams aren't lining up or your pieces are the wrong size? Suddenly, you begin losing all creative interest and feel that dreaded sense of pressure. The trick to avoiding this unpleasant experience is to be as accurate as possible from the very beginning. A firm grasp on the basics makes the entire sewing process much smoother and more enjoyable!

This approach also applies to choosing color palettes you love for your quilt projects. I don't believe there is a magic formula: color choices are personal, and a good personal color sense is developed through a daily practice of observing what we do and don't like. When you notice a beautiful flower or work of art, take time to study the various colors and identify the feelings that are inspired inside of you. Try to incorporate these observations into your fabric choices to create a stronger piece.

This book includes 28 projects featuring traditional quilting motifs, such as squares, log cabins, hexagons, diamonds, spools, and more! Each motif is accompanied by a step-by-step guide full of informative photos and useful tips. There's also a basic Japanese quilting section full of information on techniques such as fussy cutting, hand piecing, and hand quilting. No matter what type of quilter you consider yourself to be, I hope you find inspiration in this book!

Sanae Kono

CONTENTS

SQUARES

Squares are the fundamental element of all patchwork designs. They provide an excellent learning opportunity for perfecting your sewing skills. Though they may be simple, squares are extremely versatile—you can create countless quilt designs using this one classic shape.

THE SQUARE PATCH QUILT

If you're new to quilting, this project is a wonderful place to start. In fact, step-by-step photos for this quilt are included in the guide on pages 48-50. Although the construction of this quilt is quite simple, special details like the orange peel quilting motif and creative use of large-scale floral prints combine to create a sophisticated little quilt.

Instructions on page 48

THE PATCHWORK POUCH

This sweet little pouch makes the perfect case for credit cards, receipts, or even a small camera or phone. Composed of ¾ in (2 cm) squares, this project is perfect for using up your scrap stash.

Instructions on page 76

SQUARE ZIP CASE

This versatile pouch can be used as a tablet holder, mat, or stylish clutch. For a more modern look, use a large-scale floral print for one side of the pouch—it will provide interesting contrast with the patchwork.

Instructions on page 78

NINE PATCH TOTE

The nine patch is one of the most quintessential square patchwork designs. Simple nine patches and solid squares quilted with a cross motif combine to create a tote bag that's both functional and beautiful.

Instructions on page 80

TIC TAC TOE PILLOW

This dynamic pillow is a study in contrasts. In addition to a square patchwork motif, the design also incorporates circular quilting and floral print fabrics.

Instructions on page 86

SPARKLING DIAMONDS QUILT

Rows of colorful diamonds sparkle against a neutral background in this traditional quilt design. Special details, such as an embroidered border and scalloped binding add a unique touch.

Instructions on page 84

LOG CABINS

The log cabin pattern was popularized during the pioneer days, when it served as a symbol of home and warmth. Red fabric was often used for the block's center piece and symbolized the hearth, while the surrounding strips of fabric represented logs. Although the log cabin is a traditional quilting motif, blocks and fabrics can be arranged in unique ways to create more modern impressions.

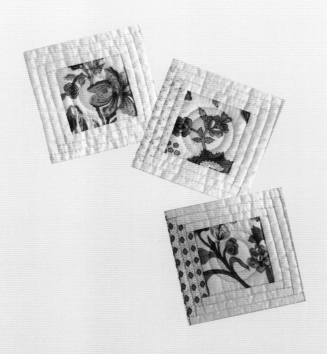

GARDEN TAPESTRY

Give this simple courthouse steps quilt pattern a twist! This design uses a floral print for the center of each block, then mixes red prints and neutral solids for the strips. The result is an intentionally asymmetric interpretation of a classic design.

Instructions on page 88

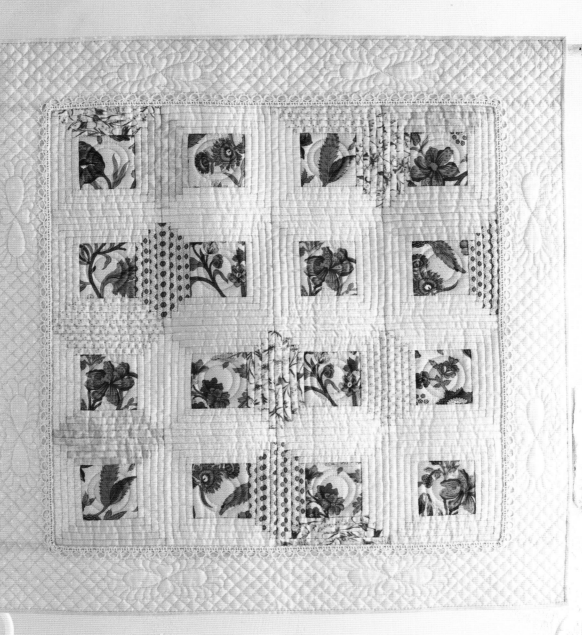

LOG CABIN GUSSET BAG

This design is perfect for those large-scale floral prints normally reserved for quilt borders and backings. Use detailed quilting to really make the flowers pop, then add a log cabin gusset for a touch of patchwork.

Instructions on page 90

LOG CABIN FLOOR MAT

With a patchwork border and simple whole cloth center, this mini quilt showcases the versatility of the log cabin block. Use it as a bedside rug, table runner, or tapestry...the possibilities are endless!

Instructions on page 93

COURTHOUSE STEPS TOTE

The large-scale rose print fabric provides an interesting contrast to the geometric log cabin blocks in this classic tote bag design. For added depth, use four different fabrics for each courthouse steps block, then arrange so like fabrics join together at the block intersections to create a larger pattern.

Instructions on page 95

MARKET TOTE

Create a dynamic diamond pattern by using four different fabrics for each log cabin block, then arranging the blocks so like fabrics align to reveal sparkling shapes. This bag features a wide gusset, making it the perfect companion for trips to the market.

Instructions on page 98

HEXAGONS

Hexagons remind me of mosaic tiles—these little polygons can be combined to create amazingly intricate designs. I'm not the only quilter with affection for hexies—the hexagon has been a popular motif throughout the history of quilting. "Grandmother's Flower Garden," which features hexagon flowers, is one of the most beloved quilting motifs of all time. Grab a needle and thread and try your hand at the hexie...I guarantee you won't be able to make just one!

FLORAL HEXAGON MATS

These versatile designs can be used as table runners, placemats, or my personal favorite: keyboard and mouse covers. I used varying shades of red for the flower petals and a creamy neutral for the centers, then selected a subtle toile print fabric for the mat center. Step-by-step photos illustrating how to make these mats from start to finish can be found in the Hexagon Techniques section.

Instructions on page 59

BLOOMING HEXIES MINI QUILT

Create floral motifs of varying sizes, then appliqué to a simple background fabric to create this dimensional wall hanging. Mount the finished quilt in a frame for a vintage look.

Instructions on page 101

APPLIQUÉD HEXIE POUCH

Appliqué a pretty hexagon flower and a few fussy cut fabric patches to transform a simple pouch into a one-of-a-kind work of art. You can even add rickrack and rhinestones for a special touch. A leaf-shaped bottom allows for extra storage space.

Instructions on page 103

HEXIES & STRIPES TAPESTRY

This quilt pattern is perfect for those beautiful border print fabrics. Alternate vertical stripes with columns of appliquéd hexie flowers for a visually striking design.

Instructions on page 106

HEXIE POCKET
MINI TOTE

This petite tote features a fun hexie panel pocket, making it a great little bag for storing a knitting or small sewing project.

Instructions on page 108

ROSETTE BASKET BAG

Perfect for special occasions, this one-of-a-kind bag features a unique shape, luxurious faux fur trim, and a detachable rosette corsage.

Instructions on page 111

DIAMONDS

Diamonds are such a versatile shape—they can be joined together to create so many unique patterns, including stars, hexagons, and arrows. With their straight lines and simple angles, diamonds are an excellent starting point for English paper piecing novices.

DIAMONDS & LACE POUCH

This elegant pouch features diamond patchwork embellished with accents of linen, lace, and beads, and is perfect for transporting your jewelry and cosmetics.

Instructions on page 118

TWINKLING STARS TABLE MAT

Combine diamonds and hexagons to create a ring of six-pointed stars. A pretty lace border adds a feminine touch to this petite table mat, designed for the top of a bureau or dressing table.

Instructions on page 121

STAR MINI QUILT

Appliqué six-pointed stars to simple squares to create this graphic mini quilt. This small quilt makes a beautiful table topper or wall hanging.

Instructions on page 123

APPLE CORES

Apple cores are named for their uniquely curved shape. The inner and outer curves are equal in length, allowing the apple cores to nest together perfectly. Sewing curves may seem intimidating, but the English paper piecing method makes the construction process a breeze.

BOW TIE CLUTCH

This sophisticated clutch features a variety of yarn-dyed fabrics in a stunning neutral color palette. Add a dramatic bow for an elegant finish.

Instructions on page 125

APPLE CORE TOTE

This beautiful bag features several unique construction details, including a sturdy hexagon-shaped bottom and curved opening bound with bias tape. This structured bag makes a great everyday carryall.

Instructions on page 128

APPLE CORE
MINI PURSE

A cream color scheme highlights the unique shape of the apple cores in this sweet mini purse. Special details like yoyo flowers and rhinestone embellishments add a stylish finish to this bag.

Instructions on page 132

APPLIQUÉ

Once you know how to appliqué, you can create almost any design with fabric. Appliqué is done by cutting fabric into unique shapes, then sewing the pieces onto a background fabric. Floral motifs are a traditional appliqué design.

ROSE PILLOW

This motif features a beautiful blooming rose at the center with rosebuds extending in all directions. A flying geese patchwork border and lace trim add a special touch to this lovely pillow.

Instructions on page 71

FLOWER PATCH MINI QUILT

This petite quilt features the same rose appliqué design from the pillow on page 33, but on a smaller scale. In fact, it's a wonderful opportunity to perfect your hand appliqué skills!

Instructions on page 134

BRODERIE PERSE

Broderie perse, or "Persian embroidery," gained popularity in 19th century England. Many women admired the exotic chintz fabrics from India which featured beautiful flowers and plants, but were unable to afford such expensive fabric. They replicated the look by cutting scraps of inexpensive fabric and appliquéing them to a piece of background fabric to create elaborate designs. This technique is created using buttonhole stitch.

BOXY BRODERIE BAG

Use broderie perse to add a beautiful floral embellishment to a simple bag silhouette. This bag features a unique construction technique in which the pieces are sewn together to create a flat cross. Next, the edges are bound, then joined together to form a three-dimensional box.

Instructions on page 136

FLORAL LACE BASKET BAG

Black lace and a rich floral print fabric combine to create this dramatic, romantic bag. The bag's round shape provides both durability and function.

Instructions on page 139

GARDEN ROWS QUILT

This stunning quilt combines broderie perse floral appliqués with simple rectangle piecing to create a design inspired by a neatly planted garden. Use low volume prints for the patchwork blocks to ensure that the floral appliqués pop.

Instructions on page 143

TOOLS & MATERIALS

Selecting the proper tools is one of the most important parts of the quilting process and will help achieve neater finished projects. The following guide lists my favorite basic quilting supplies.

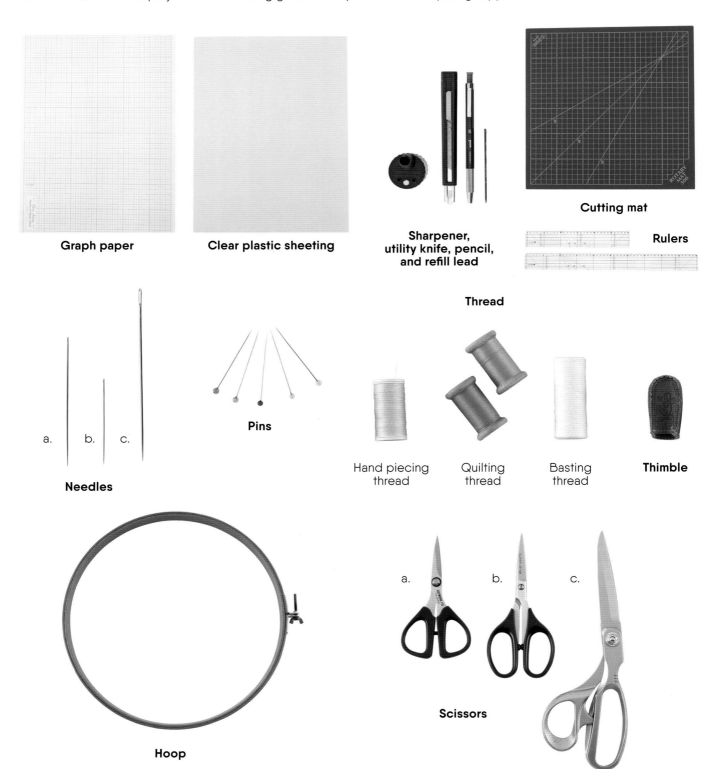

Graph paper

Clear plastic sheeting

Sharpener, utility knife, pencil, and refill lead

Cutting mat

Rulers

Thread

Needles

a. b. c.

Pins

Hand piecing thread

Quilting thread

Basting thread

Thimble

Hoop

Scissors

a. b. c.

Design boards

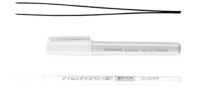

**Tweezer, glue pen,
and fabric marker**

Weights

Graph paper: Use to make templates. Look for a heavy-weight paper with ¼ in (5 mm) squares.

Clear plastic sheeting: Use to make durable, reusable templates, especially for fussy cutting fabrics.

Pencil: Use to make templates and to mark fabric. Keep your pencil sharp—use a sharpener or have refill lead on hand.

Utility knife: Use to cut templates out of clear plastic sheeting.

Cutting mat: Use a self-healing cutting mat for cutting out templates and fabric.

Rulers: Use to measure and mark templates and fabric. A 12 in (30 cm) ruler works well for small pieces, while a 20 in (50 cm) ruler is useful for large pieces.

Needles: Use the appropriately-sized needle for each job.

    a. Piecing needle: Use a medium-sized needle when hand piecing patchwork fabric.

    b. Quilting needle: Use a short, narrow needle to make tiny, accurate stitches.

    c. Basting needle: Use a long, thick needle to travel through the layers of the quilt sandwich.

Pins: Use to hold fabric pieces together while stitching.

Thread: Use 50-weight thread for hand piecing and 28-weight thread for hand quilting. You can use a neutral color for hand piecing, but make sure to match your thread color and fabric color for hand quilting and appliqué. For basting, use a lightweight thread that breaks easily for removal. You may want to use a contrasting color to your fabric so it's easy to see for removal purposes.

Thimble: Use to protect your fingers during hand piecing and quilting. Wear a leather thimble on the middle finger of our dominant hand to push the needle through the fabric and a metal thimble on the index finger of your other hand to receive the needle.

Hoop: When working on quilts larger than 40 in (1 m), use a hoop to hand quilt individual areas at a time.

Weights: Use weights when quilting smaller works and to hold your quilts in place during the basting process.

Scissors: Never cut paper with your fabric scissors.

    a. Thread snips: Use to cut threads.

    b. Small scissors: Use to cut small pieces and to trim seam allowances.

    c. Fabric shears: Use to cut fabric.

Design boards: Use design boards or a design wall to lay your pieces out before assembling your quilt. You can buy ready-made ones or create your own using quilt batting—your fabric pieces will cling to the quilt batting.

Fabric marker: Use a chalk pen or erasable marker to mark your fabric.

Glue pen: Use to hold seam allowances in place during English paper piecing and appliqué. Glue pens designed especially for use with fabric make the process neat and tidy.

Tweezer: Use bent tip tweezers to manipulate tricky areas of appliqué designs and to remove papers during English paper piecing.

BASIC JAPANESE QUILTING TECHNIQUES

Japanese quilting celebrates the art of making an object by hand and utilizes many traditional quilting techniques. The following guide presents some unique Japanese quilting tips and tricks that you may find helpful and interesting, even if you're a veteran quilter.

CUTTING YOUR FABRIC

You'll find specific cutting instructions for each project in this book. Sometimes, you'll be required to measure out and cut your fabric pieces. Seam allowance is always included when cutting dimensions are provided. Other times, you'll be provided with templates to trace. In true Japanese quilting style, seam allowance is not included in the templates. After tracing the template, you'll need to measure and mark the required seam allowance before cutting out the fabric. The following guide illustrates this process:

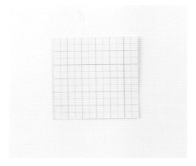

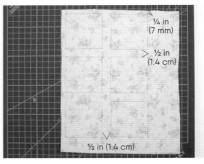

1. Trace the template from the pattern sheet. You may find it helpful to use graph paper for geometric templates. Cut the template out along the traced lines.

2. Align the template on the wrong side of the fabric and trace.

3. If you're tracing multiple templates, leave ½ in (1.4 cm) space between each one. That way, you can cut halfway between each piece and end up with ¼ in (7 mm) seam allowance for each.

A Note on Fussy Cutting

Many of the projects in this book feature fussy cut fabric pieces, where a specific area of the fabric print is intentionally selected for cutting. The following guide shows how to make a clear plastic template for fussy cutting.

1. Trace the template onto clear plastic sheeting. Use a utility knife to cut out the template.

2. Align the clear plastic template on the right side of the fabric to select the area that will be fussy cut.

3. Mark the cutting line by measuring ¼ in (7 mm) away from each edge of the template. This will be the seam allowance.

4. Completed view of the marked cutting lines.

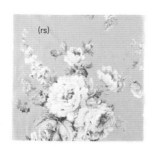

5. Cut out along the marked lines.

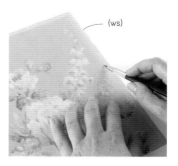

6. Trace the template onto the wrong side of the cut fabric to mark the stitching lines.

7. Completed view of a fussy cut piece with marked stitching lines.

HAND PIECING

The majority of the projects in this book were hand pieced. Hand piecing is very popular in Japan because it often allows for greater accuracy when working with small pieces. However, all of the projects in this book can be pieced by machine. The following guide illustrates the hand piecing process step-by-step.

1. Pin pieces with right sides together, matching the marked stitching lines. Make sure to insert pins at the beginning and end of the seam.

2. Knot your thread. Starting from above, insert the needle through the fabric about 1/16 in (2 mm) from the edge. Bring the needle back up through the fabric, making one stitch. Insert the needle back through the same hole as the knot.

3. Draw the needle out through the same hole as step 2 to complete the backstitch. Use a running stitch to sew along the marked line. Each stitch should measure about 1/16 in (2 mm) and look the same on both sides.

4. Use your thumb to smooth out the completed line of stitching.

5. When you reach the edge of the fabric, make one backstitch.

6. Make a French knot to secure the seam, then cut the thread. Completed view of two pieces sewn from edge to edge.

7. Fold along the seam.

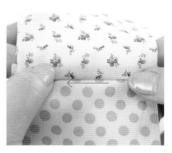

8. Open and finger press the seam.

HOW TO SEW INSET SEAMS

There are two basic hand piecing techniques used in this book: sewing from edge to edge and sewing from mark to mark. Sewing from edge to edge, as shown on page 41, is more common. Sewing from mark to mark uses inset seams and allows you to create more complicated designs.

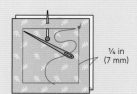

¼ in (7 mm)

1. Pin two pieces with right sides together, making sure the lines match up. Knot your thread. Starting from above, insert the needle through the fabric at the corner mark. Bring the needle back up through the fabric, making one stitch.

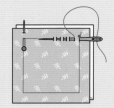

2. Insert the needle back through the same hole as the knot and draw it out through the same hole as step 1 to complete the backstitch. Use a running stitch to sew along the marked line.

3. When you reach the corner mark, make one backstitch and then secure with a French knot.

PREPARING TO QUILT

Once your quilt top is complete, you'll need to take a few steps to prepare it for the quilting process. You may be eager to get started quilting, but don't skip these steps! Taking the time to carefully mark your quilting lines and then baste the layers of the quilt together will ensure a beautifully finished quilt.

Marking Quilting Lines

Before you assemble your quilt sandwich, you'll want to mark quilting lines on your quilt top. Marking the quilt top now will allow you to draw smooth, accurate lines without the interference of batting or basting threads. The following guide shows how to mark quilting lines by using paper templates and by measuring them out with a ruler.

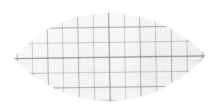

1. If your individual project includes a quilting template, make a paper template of the design.

2. Trace the template to mark the quilting design on the right side of the quilt.

3. If your individual project includes geometric quilting designs, use a ruler to mark the quilting lines on the right side of the quilt.

Basting

Although temporary in nature, basting is one of the most important steps in the quilt making process. Basting holds all the layers together while you quilt and ensures a smooth finish free of wrinkles or lumps. This traditional thread basting method is especially important if you'll be hand quilting—basting stitches allow the quilt to sit nicely in a hoop, unlike bulky safety pins used in pin basting methods. The following guide outlines the basting process from start to finish:

1. Lay your backing fabric on a flat surface with the wrong side facing up. Smooth out the fabric, starting from the center and working toward the edges. Tip: If you're working on a table, you may want to use duct tape to prevent the fabric from moving. If you're working on a rug, use safety pins.

2. Align the batting on top of the backing. Use the same process to smooth out the batting.

3. With the right side facing up, align the quilt top on the batting. Use the same process to smooth out the fabric.

4. Place weights on top of the fabric to hold the quilt in place while you work.

5. Use long tacking stitches to baste the layers of the quilt together. Start at the center and work toward the edges, following the numerical order indicated by the pink arrows. Take care to avoid the seams and quilting lines.

6. Baste along the seam lines where the border connects to the patchwork and along the finishing lines around the perimeter of the quilt, as indicated by the green arrows.

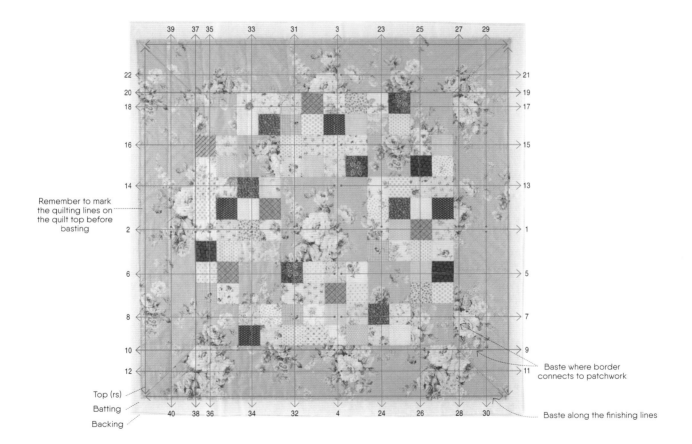

Remember to mark the quilting lines on the quilt top before basting

Baste where border connects to patchwork

Baste along the finishing lines

Top (rs)
Batting
Backing

Note: The batting and backing should be cut about 6 in (15 cm) larger than quilt top for large projects and about 4 in (10 cm) larger than the quilt top for small projects. The extra fabric will compensate for any shifting that occurs during the quilting process and will be trimmed down before the binding is attached. This extra fabric is included in the batting and backing cutting dimensions for each project.

HAND QUILTING

The majority of the projects in this book were hand quilted. Hand quilting is very popular in Japan because it often allows for more complex motifs. The following guide illustrates the hand quilting process step-by-step.

1. Starting from the center, insert the quilt into a large hoop.

2. Adjust the tension: Press the fabric to loosen the tension or turn the screws to tighten.

3. Knot your thread. Insert the needle into the quilt top and batting a short distance away from where you will start quilting. Draw the needle out at the starting point.

4. Pull the thread to bring the knot through the quilt top and hide it inside the batting.

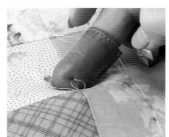

5. With a thimble positioned on the middle finger of your dominant hand, vertically insert the needle through all three layers of the quilt. Use the index finger of your other hand to receive the needle underneath the quilt, then push it back up through all three layers of the quilt. Repeat this process 3–5 times before pulling the thread through the quilt.

Tip: You may wish to wear a metal thimble on the index of the hand underneath the quilt. This will help you receive the needle and push it back up through the quilt.

HOW TO START & FINISH A THREAD WHEN QUILTING

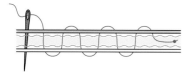

How to Start: Pull the thread taut to bring the knot through the quilt top and hide it inside the batting.

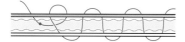

How to Finish: Make one backstitch, then make a knot. Pull the thread taut, then trim to hide the knot inside the quilt batting.

HOW TO QUILT THICK SEAMS

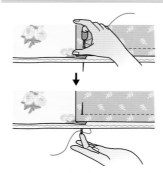

It can be difficult to quilt areas where seams intersect since there are several layers of fabric. To quilt these areas, work slowly and make one quilting stitch at a time using an up and down motion.

HOW TO STITCH IN THE DITCH

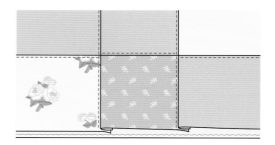

Many of the designs in this book call for "stitching in the ditch." To stitch in the ditch, quilt as close to the seam as possible, making sure to quilt the side without the seam allowance.

BINDING A QUILT

In Japan, quilts are often finished with single-fold bias binding. The following guide shows how to cut bias strips, sew them together into a binding, then attach the binding to the quilt.

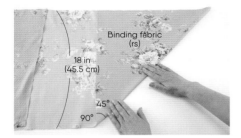

1. Cut a rectangular piece of fabric to use for the bias strips. You'll need about ½ yd (0.5 m) for small projects and 1 yd (1 m) for larger quilts. Fold as shown to create a 45° angle, then crease.

2. Unfold the fabric. Align your ruler with the crease line on the wrong side of the fabric and mark the diagonal line.

3. Continue marking diagonal lines parallel to the crease. The distance between the lines should be equal to the desired cut width of your bias strips.

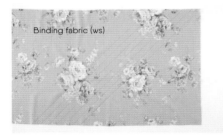

4. Mark as many strips as necessary for the binding. Cut along the diagonal lines to make strips.

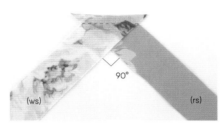

5. Align the short edges of two strips with right sides together, forming a 90° angle. Sew along the short edges to attach the strips.

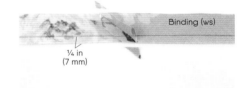

6. Sew all the strips together, press open, then trim the excess fabric. On the wrong side, mark the stitch line along one long edge.

7. Before attaching the binding to the quilt, trim the excess batting and backing to match the quilt top. This should include ¼ in (7 mm) seam allowance for attaching the binding.

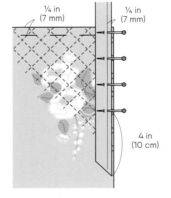

8. With right sides together, align binding and quilt top, matching up the marked stitch lines. Pin together, leaving the first 4 in (10 cm) unattached. Stop pinning when you reach the first corner.

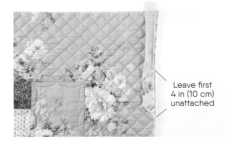

9. Backstitch, then sew toward the corner. Stop sewing ¼ in (7 mm) from the corner. Backstitch, then cut the thread.

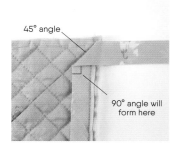

10. Fold the binding away from the quilt at a 45° angle.

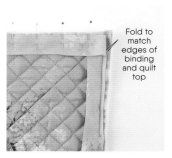

11. Fold the binding back down to match the edges of the quilt top. Pin in place. Start ¼ in (7 mm) from the corner and continue sewing along the next side of the quilt.

12. Use this process to sew the binding to all four sides of the quilt. On the last side, stop sewing 4 in (10 cm) from the start of the binding. Align the end of the binding as shown, then fold the excess away from the quilt.

13. Cut the excess binding, leaving ½ in (1.4 cm) seam allowance.

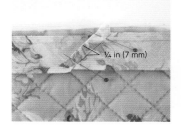

14. Align the short edges of the binding with right sides together. Sew, using ¼ in (7 mm) seam allowance.

15. Trim the excess and press the seam allowance open.

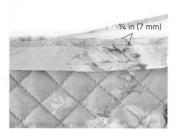

16. Sew the unattached portion of the binding to the quilt top. Trim any excess fabric and batting if necessary.

17. Wrap the binding around the seam allowances to the back of the quilt. Fold the raw edge under. Start hand stitching the binding to the backing, hiding the seam line.

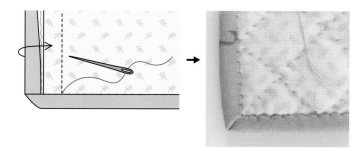

18. Stop at the corner seam line. Fold the next side of the binding to create a mitered corner. Continue sewing the binding to the backing to complete the quilt.

SQUARE TECHNIQUES

Squares are the foundation of patchwork quilting and make an excellent starting point for beginners. Refer to the Basic Japanese Quilting Techniques on page 40 for tips on how to cut and hand piece squares. The following guide includes a few helpful tips specific to square-themed projects.

HOW TO PIN SQUARE PIECES

It's important to accurately pin square pieces in order to ensure that the seams align once the pieces are sewn together. The following photos illustrate how to match seams and use pins to hold everything in place while sewing.

Pinning Pieces Together

Pinning Rows Together

1. Align two squares with right sides together. Insert a pin at the beginning of the seam, matching up the marked stitching lines.

2. Insert a pin at the end of the seam as well.

1. First, insert the pin through the top layer of fabric, just to the right of the seam.

2. Next, insert the pin through the bottom layer of fabric, just to the left of the seam. When pinning the bottom layer, use the pin to hold in the seam allowance in place underneath.

HOW TO PRESS THE SEAM ALLOWANCES OF SQUARE PIECES

After square pieces have been sewn together, it's important to press the seam allowances in the proper direction so that the quilt top will lie flat once it's assembled. If seam allowances aren't pressed in the correct direction, it may result in a lumpy quilt top. For rows of square patchwork, press seam allowances in one direction for odd rows and the opposite direction for even rows. Positioning the seams so they face away from each other will reduce bulk once the rows are sewn together.

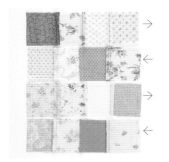
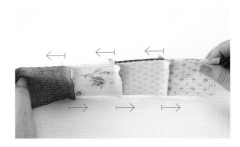

1. Press the seam allowances in opposite directions for alternating rows.

2. When adjacent rows are aligned, the short seam allowances should face opposite directions as indicated by the red arrows.

3. Press the long seam allowances in the same direction as you sew the rows together.

SQUARE EXAMPLE PROJECT

The following guide uses **The Square Patch Quilt** (shown on page 7) as an example to illustrate common square techniques. Many of these techniques are used for the other square projects in the book.

Materials

- **Main fabric (for patchwork, borders, and binding):** 1¾ yds (1.6 m) of gray floral print
- **Patchwork fabric:** 20 assorted red, pink, and beige prints
- **Backing fabric:** 1½ yds (1.4 m)
- **Batting:** 46½ in (118 cm) square

Sew using ¼ in (7 mm) seam allowance, unless otherwise noted.

Project Diagram

Diagram shows finished measurements (seam allowance not included).

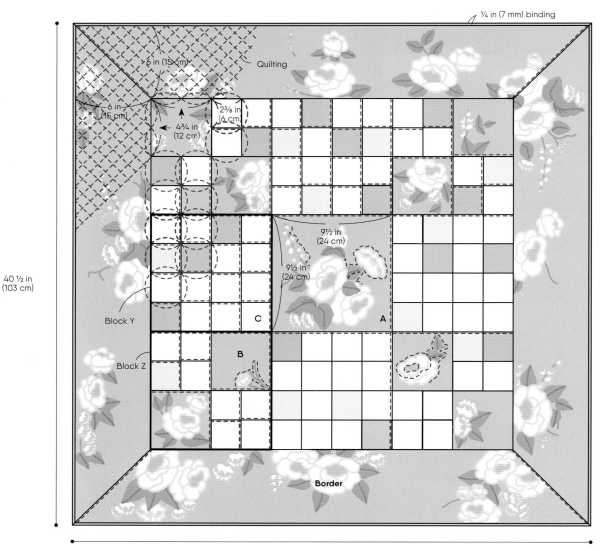

Cutting Instructions

Cut out the following fabric pieces, which do not have templates, according to the measurements below (these measurements include seam allowance).

Main fabric

- A: 10 in (25.4 cm) square
- B (cut 8): 5¼ in (13.4 cm) squares
- Borders (cut 4): 6½ x 47 in (16.4 x 119.5 cm)
- Binding: 4¾ yds (4.4 m) of 1¼ in (3 cm) wide single-fold bias binding

Assorted scraps

- C (cut 96): 2⅞ in (7.4 cm) squares

Batting

- Batting: 46½ in (118 cm) square

Backing fabric

- Backing: 46½ in (118 cm) square

Construction Steps

1. Make four of Block Y: Sew 16 C pieces together to make each Block Y (refer to page 41 for square piecing tips).

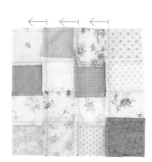

2. Make four of Block Z: Each Block Z is composed of two B pieces and eight C pieces. Sew the C pieces together to make four patches, then sew to the B pieces.

3. Sew the blocks together to make the quilt top: Sew Blocks Y, Z and piece A together, following the layout shown in the diagram on page 48.

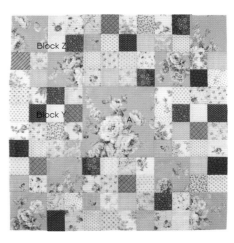

4. Mark the quilting lines on the quilt top: Make a template of the orange peel quilting motif on page 50. Align the points of the template with two corners of a square. Trace the template. Repeat along each edge of every square (trace multiples for larger squares). **Note:** You'll mark the orange peel quilting motif along the outer squares once the border has been attached in step 5.

5. Sew the mitered borders to the quilt top (refer to page 51).

6. Make marks 1¼ in (3 cm) apart along the inner edge of each border. Use the template to mark the orange peel quilting motif, overlapping both the patchwork quilt top and the border. Next, mark the rest of the borders with the crosshatch quilting lines 1¼ in (3 cm) apart.

7. Layer the top, batting, and backing. Baste the quilt as shown on page 43.

8. Use the process shown on page 44 to stitch in the ditch around the patchwork pieces and to quilt the orange peel and crosshatch quilting motifs. Finally, quilt around the floral print of the fabric on the A and B pieces.

9. Bind the quilt as shown on page 45.

Full-Size Template

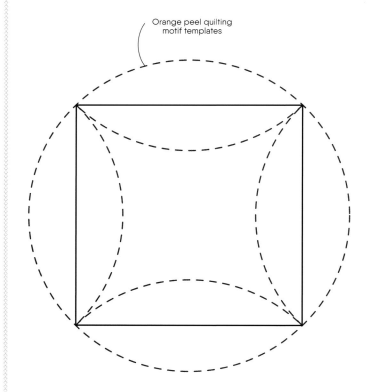

Orange peel quilting motif templates

HOW TO MAKE A MITERED BORDER

Mitered borders neatly frame a quilt top and create a clean, sharp finish. The following guide illustrates how to sew a mitered border onto your quilt top.

1. Fold both the quilt top and borders in half, then mark the centers. With right sides together, pin the borders to the quilt top, aligning the centers.

2. Sew each border to the quilt top, starting and stopping at the marked finishing line (this would be ¼ in [7 mm] from the edge of a trimmed quilt top). Make sure to backstitch at the beginning and end.

3. With right sides together, fold the quilt top in half diagonally to form a triangle. Align two adjacent borders. Position a ruler along the folded edge of the quilt top, extending at a 45° angle across the border. Mark the line on the border, then pin the two borders together.

4. Sew the miter, starting from the end of the border seam from step 2 and continuing along the marked line from step 3. Make sure the to backstitch at the beginning and end.

5. Trim the excess border fabric, leaving ¼ in (7 mm) seam allowance. Press the seam.

6. Repeat steps 3–5 to miter the other borders.

LOG CABIN TECHNIQUES

A log cabin block is made by sewing rectangular strips around a center piece of fabric. There are many different techniques for piecing log cabin blocks. The following guide shows how to hand piece a log cabin block.

BASIC LOG CABIN BLOCKS

For a basic log cabin block, sew the strips to the center in a counter-clockwise direction.

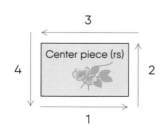

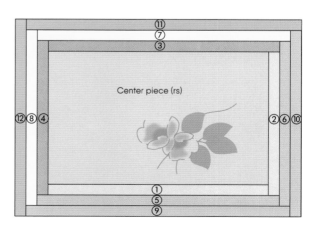

How to Cut the Center Piece

1. It's important to be precise when cutting the center piece of a log cabin block; otherwise, the entire block may end up the wrong size or be crooked. If you plan to fussy cut your center pieces, make a clear plastic template.

2. Use the plastic template to select the area of the fabric to cut.

3. Cut the center piece out, including ¼ in (7 mm) seam allowance.

How to Cut the Strips

● = ⅜ in (1 cm)
▲ = ⅝ in (1.5 cm)

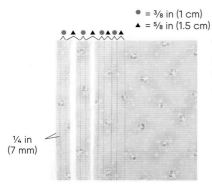

¼ in (7 mm)

1. Cut the strips out, including ¼ in (7 mm) seam allowance.

Japanese Sewing Tip: For ⅜ in (1 cm) wide finished strips, mark a line ¼ in (7 mm) from the edge of the fabric. Mark another line ⅜ in (1 cm) away (as represented by the pink ●). Finally, mark a third line ⅝ in (1.5 cm) away from the last one (as represented by the black ▲). Cut the strip halfway between the ⅜ in (1 cm) and ⅝ in (1.5 cm) lines. You will now have a strip with perfectly marked ¼ in (7 mm) seam allowances. Use the same process to mark and cut the other strips.

2. Use the templates to trim the strips to length, leaving ¼ in (7 mm) seam allowance on each end. Arrange the strips around the center piece to determine the layout.

How to Sew the Strips to the Center Piece

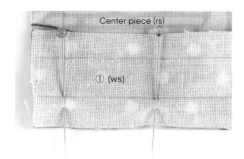

1. Pin strip ① to the bottom edge of the center piece with right sides together.

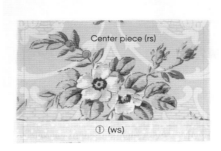

2. Sew strip ① to the bottom of the center piece. If you're hand piecing, make sure to use small stitches, about 1/16 in (2 mm).

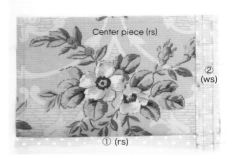

3. On the right side, press strip ① open. Pin strip ② to the right edge of the center piece with right sides together.

4. Sew strip ② to the center piece, then press strip ② open from the right side.

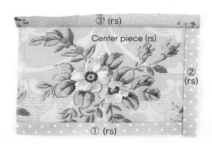

5. Use the same process to sew strip ③ to the top edge of the center piece and press it open.

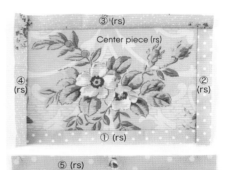

6. Use the same process to sew strip ④ to the left edge of the center piece and press it open. One round of strips has now been attached. Follow the same process to attach another round of strips, starting at the bottom.

7. Use this process to attach three rounds of strips total. Always press the seam allowances away from the center piece.

COURTHOUSE STEPS BLOCKS

A courthouse steps block is a variation on a traditional log cabin block. For a courthouse steps block, sew strips of the same length to the left and right edges of a square center piece, then to the top and bottom edges. This technique allows you to create interesting patterns and color combinations based on the layout of your blocks. The following guide uses the Garden Tapestry on page 13 as an example.

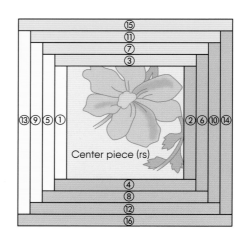

How to Cut the Center Piece

Use a clear plastic template to cut a square center piece.

How to Cut the Strips

Follow the same process used on page 52 to cut the strips. Remember, strips along the opposite edges of the center piece will have the same length. Arrange the strips around the center piece to determine the layout.

How to Sew the Strips to the Center Piece

1. With right sides together, sew strip ① to the left edge of the center piece. Press open. Use the same process to sew strip ② to the right edge of the center piece.

2. Use the same process to sew strips ③ and ④ to the top and bottom edges of the center piece. One round is now complete.

3. Use the same process to attach four rounds of strips total to complete the block. Always press the seam allowances away from the center piece.

When you sew two courthouse steps blocks together, you can create a unique diamond pattern based on the fabric layout.

HEXAGON TECHNIQUES

The hexie projects in this book were made with English paper piecing, a method in which fabric is wrapped around a paper template, then hand stitched in place to create precise geometric shapes. Because they're sewn by hand, hexies are highly portable and make great travel companions. I like to work on them in my spare time, so they're ready to go once I have time to decide upon a layout.

A Note About English Paper Piecing Templates

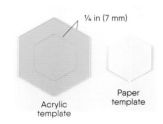

¼ in (7 mm)

Acrylic template

Paper template

There are many helpful tools available for English paper piecing hexies. I like to use an acrylic template (with removable seam allowance) to cut my hexies and paper templates to piece my hexies. Some quilters prefer to use thin paper templates for piecing, while others prefer to use thick cardstock templates. You can buy precut paper templates or make your own.

How to Cut Hexies from Fabric

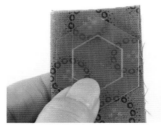

1. Fold your piece of fabric in half, then fold it into thirds as shown. This will allow you to cut six hexies at once!

2. Align the hexie template on top of the folded fabric.

3. Trim the fabric into a square to make it easier to work with while you cut.

4. Completed view of step 3.

5. Use the template as a guide to trim each side into shape. If your template doesn't include seam allowance, just eyeball ¼ in (7 mm) as you cut.

6. Completed view of step 5.

7. Carefully trim along the folds to separate the fabric layers into individual hexies.

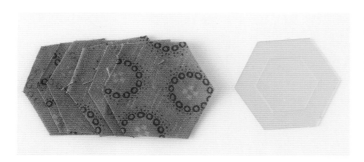

8. Six hexies are now cut out. Repeat this process until you have the desired number of hexies. It's always a good idea to have a few extras on hand.

How to Baste Hexies

(ws)   (rs)

1. Apply a small dab of glue to the center of the hexie on the wrong side of the fabric. Adhere a paper hexie template to the center of the fabric.

2. Fold the seam allowance along one side, wrapping it around the paper template. Insert the needle through the fabric and paper template.

3. Fold the seam allowance along the next side. Insert the needle back through the fabric where the seam allowances overlap.

4. Repeat steps 2 and 3 to baste the fabric around the paper template on all sides.

How to Sew Hexies Together

1. Arrange the hexies into the desired layout. Many hexie motifs feature a flower with a center and six petals.

2. Align two petals with right sides together. Insert the needle through both hexies, about three stitches away from the corner. Take care not to insert the needle through the paper template.

3. Draw the needle through the fabric. Make another stitch toward the corner, inserting the needle through the hexie farthest from you first. This is called the whipstitch (see below).

4. Make sure the corners of the two hexies are aligned. Make your third stitch right at the corner.

5. Reverse direction, then continue using the whipstitch to sew the two hexies together, working toward the opposite corner.

6. Once you've reached the opposite corner, reverse direction and make 2–3 more whipstitches. Make a French knot to secure.

7. Completed view of two hexies whipstitched together.

HOW TO WHIPSTITCH

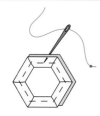 

1. Align two hexies with right sides together. Insert the needle through both hexies, about three stitches away from the corner. Take care not to insert the needle through the paper template.

2. Draw the needle through the fabric. Make another stitch toward the corner, inserting the needle through the hexie farthest from you first.

3. Make one more stitch at the corner, then reverse direction. Continue stitching until your reach the opposite corner.

4. Reverse direction and make 2–3 more stitches. Secure with a French knot.

8. Repeat steps 2–7 to make three sets composed of two hexie petals each.

9. Next, you'll sew the petal sets to the flower center.

10. Align the first petal and the flower center with right sides together. Insert the needle through both hexies, about three stitches away from the corner.

11. Repeat steps 2–5 to sew the two hexies together to the corner.

12. When you reach the corner, align the flower center and the second petal with right sides together.

13. Whipstitch these two hexies with right sides together. **Note:** It may help to fold the first petal as shown to make it easier to sew.

14. Completed view of the first two petals joined to the flower center.

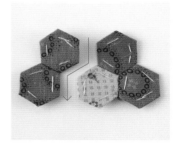

15. Use the same process to sew the next set of petals to the flower center.

16. Sew the final set of petals to the flower center.

17. Completed view of one flower motif. Make as many flower motifs as necessary.

The following guide uses the **Floral Hexagon Mats** (shown on page 19) as an example to illustrate common hexagon techniques. Many of these techniques are used for the other hexagon projects in the book.

Project Diagram

Diagrams show finished measurements (seam allowance not included).

Small Mat

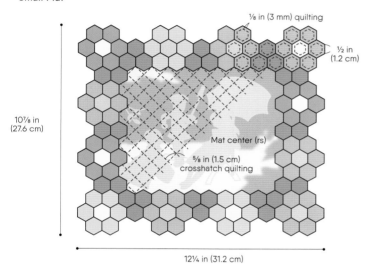

Large Mat

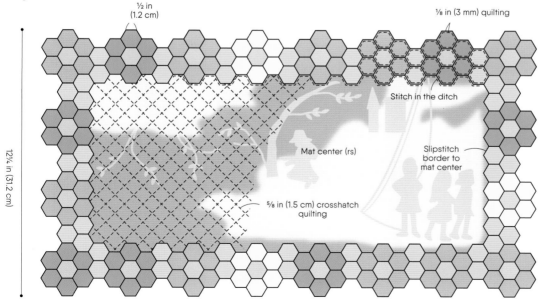

Materials

FOR THE SMALL MAT

- **Hexagon fabric:** 10–15 assorted scraps
- **Mat center fabric:** One fat eighth of toile fabric
- **Backing fabric:** One fat quarter
- **Batting:** 15 x 16¼ in (37.6 x 41.2 cm)
- (114) ½ in (1.2 cm) hexagon precut EPP shapes

FOR THE LARGE MAT

- **Hexagon fabric:** 10–15 assorted scraps
- **Mat center fabric:** One fat quarter of toile fabric
- **Backing fabric:** ½ yd (0.5 m)
- **Batting:** 16¼ x 25¾ in (41.2 x 65.2 cm)
- (186) ½ in (1.2 cm) hexagon precut EPP shapes

Sew using ¼ in (7 mm) seam allowance, unless otherwise noted.

Full-Size Template

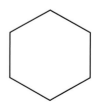

Note: This template should be used for piecing the hexies. Add ¼ in (7 mm) seam allowance to cut out each hexie.

Cutting Instructions

SMALL MAT

Trace and cut out the template on page 59. Cut out the following fabric pieces, adding ¼ in (7 mm) seam allowance:

Hexagon fabric

- 114 hexagons

Cut out the following fabric pieces, which do not have templates, according to the measurements below (these measurements include seam allowance).

Mat center fabric

- Mat center: 9 x 10½ in (22.8 x 26.8 cm)

Batting

- Batting: 15 x 16¼ in (37.6 x 41.2 cm)

Backing fabric

- Backing: 15 x 16¼ in (37.6 x 41.2 cm)

LARGE MAT

Trace and cut out the template on page 59. Cut out the following fabric pieces, adding ¼ in (7 mm) seam allowance:

Hexagon fabric

- 186 hexagons

Cut out the following fabric pieces, which do not have templates, according to the measurements below (these measurements include seam allowance).

Mat center fabric

- Mat center: 10½ x 20 in (26.8 x 50.4 cm)

Batting

- Batting: 16¼ x 25¾ in (41.2 x 65.2 cm)

Backing fabric

- Backing: 16¼ x 25¾ in (41.2 x 65.2 cm)

Construction Steps

1. Make the required number of hexies as shown in the guide on page 55.

	Hexies
Small Mat	114
Large Mat	186

2. Sew the hexies together into the required number of flower motifs as shown in the guide on page 57.

	Flower Motifs
Small Mat	12
Large Mat	20

3. You'll also need sets of two hexies and sets of three hexies for in between the flowers. Use the remaining hexies to make the required number of sets.

	Sets of 2	Sets of 3
Small Mat	6	6
Large Mat	14	6

4. Make the border: Arrange the flower motifs and hexie sets as shown in the diagram on page 59. Whipstitch the border together.

Hexie Tips

Once the border is complete, press it from the wrong side. Remove the basting stitches and paper templates.

Use a glue pen to stabilize any seam allowances that are not secure.

5. Prepare the mat center: Mark the quilting and finishing lines on the right side of the mat center (**Note:** The mat center is 1 ¼ in [3 cm] larger than the inside border dimensions along each side).

6. Baste the mat center to the border: Align the border on top of the mat center. Baste in place, taking care not to shift the mat center as you work.

7. Slipstitch the inner edges of the border to the mat center.

8. Once the entire border has been slipstitched, flip the mat over to the wrong side. Trim the excess center fabric, leaving ¼ in (7 mm) seam allowance.

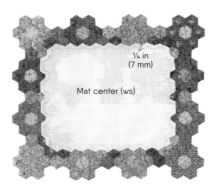

9. Arrange the backing fabric with the wrong side facing up. Lay the batting and mat on top with the right side facing up. Baste all three layers together using the same process shown on page 43.

10. Quilt the mat center with a crosshatch motif, then quilt the hexies using ⅛ in (3 mm) seam allowance. Do not quilt the hexies along the outer edges of the mat—these will be quilted once the edges are finished.

11. Trim the backing and batting so they are ¼ in (7 mm) larger than the mat top along each side.

12. Next, trim the batting only, so it matches the size and shape of the mat top. Do not trim the backing.

13. Make clips into the backing at the concave hexagon corners, as shown in the diagram below. Stop clipping about 1 mm from the finishing line (marked in blue).

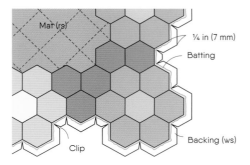

14. Use your needle tip to fold the backing seam allowance in so it aligns with the mat top. Hold the layers of fabric together using your thumb and fingers.

15. Slipstitch the mat top and backing together.

16. Use this process to finish the edges of the mat, working with small sections at a time.

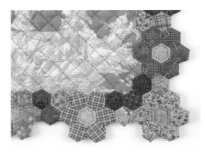

17. Quilt the hexies along the outer edges of the mat that were left unquilted earlier.

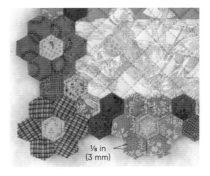

DIAMOND TECHNIQUES

Diamonds are incredibly versatile shapes—they can be arranged in several different ways to create various patterns. The following guide shows how to make diamonds with English paper piecing, then sew them together.

A Note About English Paper Piecing Templates

¼ in
(7 mm)

Acrylic
template

Paper
template

There are many helpful tools available for English paper piecing diamonds. I like to use an acrylic template (with removable seam allowance) to cut my diamonds and paper templates to piece my diamonds. Some quilters prefer to use thin paper templates for piecing, while others prefer to use thick cardstock templates. You can buy precut paper templates or make your own.

How to English Paper Piece Diamonds

Width of cutting template

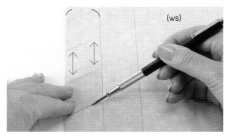

1. Draw vertical guidelines matching the width of your diamonds (including seam allowance) on the wrong side of the fabric. Align your cutting template with the guidelines and trace.

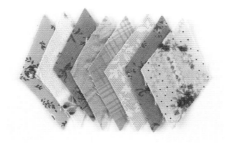

2. Cut the diamonds out along the marked lines.

3. Apply a small dab of glue to the center of the diamond on the wrong side of the fabric.

4. Adhere a paper diamond template to the center of the fabric. Fold the seam allowance along one side, wrapping it around the paper template.

5. Trim the excess fabric that extends beyond the seam allowance.

6. Fold the seam allowance along the next side. Fold the extended corner so that it overlaps with the first side of the diamond (see the next photo).

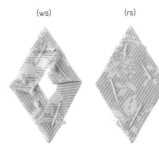

(ws)   (rs)

7. Completed view of the folded corner.

8. Baste in place, continuing to fold the seam allowances around the paper template as you work. Make sure to insert the needle through the folded corners to hold the layers of fabric in place.

9. Completed view of an English paper pieced diamond.

How to Sew into a Diamond

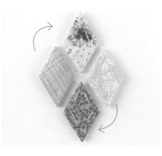

1. Arrange four diamonds as shown. Baste each diamond around a paper template as shown on page 63.

2. The arrows indicate how the diamonds will be sewn together in sets.

3. Align two diamonds with right sides together. Whip-stitch them together along one side (refer to page 57).

4. When you reach the end, make sure the corners of the two diamonds are aligned. Reverse direction and make a couple more stitches before securing with a knot.

5. Repeat steps 3 and 4 to sew the other set of diamonds together.

6. Align the two sets with right sides together. Start stitching the two sets together.

7. Make sure the four corners are aligned before you stitch the centers together.

8. Completed view of four diamonds stitched together into a larger diamond.

How to Sew into a Star

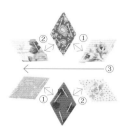

1. Arrange six diamonds as shown. Baste each diamond around a paper template as shown on page 63.

2. Whipstitch the diamonds together as indicated by the arrows and numerical order listed above.

3. Completed view of six diamonds sewn together into a star.

How to Sew into a Panel

1. Arrange the diamonds according to your desired layout. Baste each diamond around a paper template as shown on page 63.

2. Whipstitch the diamonds together in diagonal rows.

3. Whipstitch the rows together to assemble the panel.

APPLE CORE TECHNIQUES

Apple core motifs fit together just like puzzle pieces, making them quite fun to sew. It can be difficult to imagine how the concave and convex curves will fit together, but once you lay your pieces out, the pattern will start to emerge. The following guide shows how to make apple cores with English paper piecing, then sew them together.

A Note About English Paper Piecing Templates

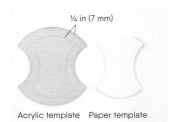

¼ in (7 mm)

Acrylic template   Paper template

There are many helpful tools available for English paper piecing apple cores. I like to use an acrylic template (with removable seam allowance) to cut my apple cores and paper templates to piece my apple cores. Some quilters prefer to use thin paper templates for piecing, while others prefer to use thick cardstock templates. You can buy precut paper templates or make your own.

How to English Paper Piece Apple Cores

1. Align your cutting template with the wrong side of the fabric so the template is positioned on the bias. This will make it easier to fold and sew the curves. Trace the template.

2. Cut the apple cores out along the marked lines.

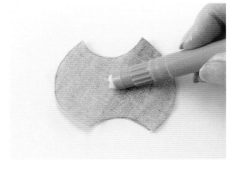

3. Apply a small dab of glue to the center of the apple core on the wrong side of the fabric.

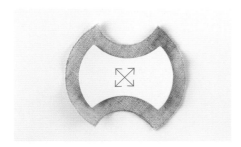

4. Adhere a paper apple core template to the center of the fabric.

5. Make three clips into the seam allowance along the concave curve.

6. Use the needle tip and your finger to fold the seam allowance, wrapping it around the paper template.

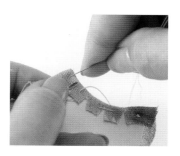

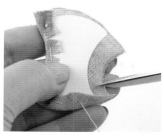

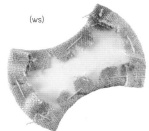

7. Begin basting the seam allowance in place. When you reach the next side, neatly fold the corner, then continue basting.

8. Make clips into the seam allowance along the other concave curve, then finish basting.

9. Completed view of an English paper pieced apple core.

How to Sew the Apple Cores Together

1. Arrange the basted apple cores according to your desired layout.

2. You'll be sewing the convex curve of one apple core to the concave curve of another. Align two apple cores with right sides together as shown.

3. Make sure the corners are aligned, then start whip-stitching the apple cores together (refer to page 57).

4. Whipstitch the apple cores with right sides together until you reach the point where the curves no longer align.

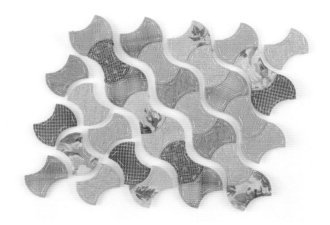

5. Open the apple cores so they lay flat, using your index finger to support the pieces. Continue whipstitching them together.

6. When you reach the end, make sure the corners of the two apple cores are aligned. Reverse direction and make a couple more stitches before securing with a knot.

7. Continue whipstitching the apple cores together in diagonal rows. Finally, whipstitch the rows together.

APPLIQUÉ TECHNIQUES

Appliqué allows you to create interesting, complex shapes with fabric that aren't always possible with patchwork techniques. Hand appliqué may seem intimidating at first, but with a little practice, you'll be able to create beautiful designs. The following guide illustrates the hand appliqué process from start to finish.

How to Make Appliqué Templates

Tip: When making templates of symmetrical motifs, first draw a set of horizontal and vertical lines intersecting at a 90° angle. This will help ensure your appliqué pieces are on the straight grain when you cut them out of fabric.

1. Trace or copy the appliqué motif template from the pattern sheet. Trace the motif onto clear plastic sheeting.

2. You'll need a separate template for each component of the motif.

3. Trace each component onto clear plastic sheeting, then cut them out.

How to Cut Appliqué Fabric

1. Align the clear plastic template on the right side of the fabric to select the area that will be cut. Trace the outline of the template.

2. Add ⅛ in (3 mm) seam allowance, then cut out. Follow the same process to cut out all the appliqué pieces.

3. Cut your background fabric out following the dimensions noted in the specific project instructions. Fold the fabric into eighths and crease to find the center. Align the center of the background fabric with the center of the appliqué motif template and pin in place.

4. Lightly trace the appliqué motif onto the right side of the background fabric.

5. Completed view of the appliqué motif traced onto the background fabric.

How to Hand Appliqué

Hold the folded seam allowance in place

1. Always start with the bottom layer of the appliqué motif. Apply a dab of glue to the background fabric, then adhere the appliqué piece.

2. Use the needle tip to fold the seam allowance under on the appliqué piece. Work in small sections at a time for smooth and precise curves.

3. Slipstitch the appliqué piece to the background fabric as shown below.

HOW TO SLIPSTITCH FOR APPLIQUÉ

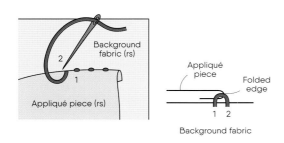

Background fabric (rs)

Appliqué piece (rs)

Appliqué piece

Folded edge

Background fabric

1. Starting from the wrong side of the background fabric, insert the needle through both layers of fabric and draw it out along the marked finishing line of the appliqué piece.

2. Insert the needle back down into the background fabric next to where you drew the needle out in step 1. Keep your stitches straight—slanted stitches tend to be more visible.

3. Without pulling the thread all the way through the fabric, bring the needle back up through both layers of fabric, a short distance away from the last stitch. Tighten your stitches as you work.

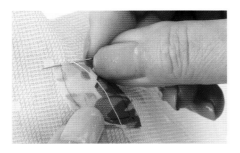

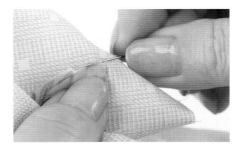

4. Continue slipstitching the appliqué piece to the background fabric. For appliqué pieces with a point, insert the needle through the appliqué piece right at the tip of the point.

5. Pull the thread through the fabric. Use the needle tip to fold the seam allowance under along the next side.

6. Insert the needle back down through the background fabric right next to the tip of the appliqué piece. Continue slipstitching around the appliqué piece.

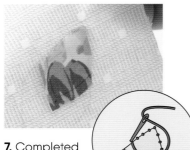

7. Completed view of the appliquéd bud. **Note:** There's no need to slipstitch the appliqué piece around edges where another piece will overlap.

8. For appliqué pieces with a V-shape, clip into the seam allowance at the point.

9. Position the appliqué piece in place and use the same process to slipstitch it to the background fabric. Always use a color of thread that matches the appliqué fabric, not the background fabric.

10. Insert the needle through the appliqué piece at the point of the V.

11. Pull the thread through the fabric. Use the needle tip to fold the seam allowance under along the next side.

12. Insert the needle back down through the background fabric right next to the V point. Continue slipstitching around the appliqué piece.

13. Use the same process to appliqué the rest of the design.

14. Completed view of the appliqué motif. Notice all the different thread colors visible on the wrong side of the work.

The following guide uses the **Rose Pillow** (shown on page 33) as an example to illustrate common appliqué techniques. Many of these techniques are used for the other appliqué projects in the book.

Materials

- **Background fabric:** One fat quarter of beige polka dot
- **Appliqué fabrics:** Four red or pink prints for flowers and one green print for leaves
- **Border fabric #1:** 13¾ in (35 cm) square of blue print
- **Border fabric #2:** Nine assorted 8 in (20 cm) square neutral prints
- **Border fabric #3:** Red and white striped scrap
- **Back fabric:** ½ yd (0.5 m) of striped fabric
- ⅝ yd (0.6 m) of muslin

- **Batting:** 19¾ in (50 cm) square
- **Lightweight fusible interfacing:** 4 x 19¾ in (10 x 50 cm)
- 2¼ yds (2 m) of 1¾ in (4.5 cm) wide lace
- Three ¾ in (2 cm) buttons
- (60) ⅜ in (1 cm) decorative buttons

> • Sew using ¼ in (7 mm) seam allowance, unless otherwise noted.
>
> • Stitch in the ditch around all appliqué and patchwork pieces.

Project Diagram

Diagrams show finished measurements (seam allowance not included).

Front

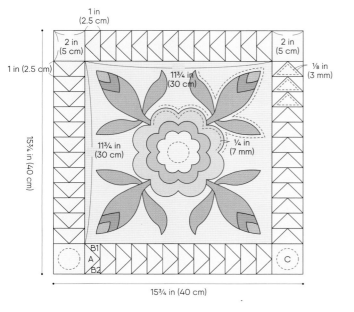

Back

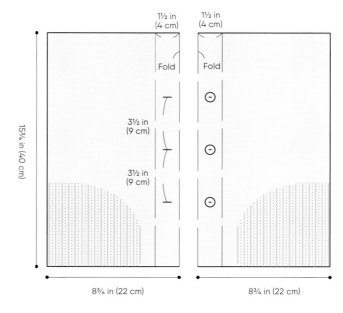

Cutting Instructions

Trace and cut out the templates on Pattern Sheet B. Cut out the following fabric pieces, adding ⅛ in (3 mm) seam allowance.

Appliqué fabrics
- Appliqué motif pieces

Cut out the following fabric pieces, adding ¼ in (7 mm) seam allowance.

Border fabric #1
- 48 A triangles

Border fabric #2
- 48 B1 triangles
- 48 B2 triangles

Cut out the following fabric pieces, which do not have templates, according to the measurements below (these measurements include seam allowance).

Background fabric
- Background: 15¾ in (40 cm) square

Border fabric #3
- C squares (cut 4): 2½ in (6.4 cm)

Batting
- Pillow batting: 19¾ in (50 cm) square

Muslin
- Muslin base: 19¾ in (50 cm) square

Back fabric
- Backs: (cut 2): 9¼ x 16¼ in (23.4 x 41.4 cm)

Fusible interfacing
- Fusible interfacing strips (cut 2): 1½ x 16¼ in (4 x 41.4 cm)

Construction Steps

1. Appliqué the motif onto the background fabric as shown in the guide on page 68. Mark the finishing lines and trim down to size, leaving ¼ in (7 mm) seam allowance.

2. Make the flying geese borders: Sew a B1 piece and a B2 piece to each A piece as shown. Sew 12 of these sets together for each border. Make four borders.

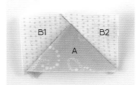

3. Sew the vertical borders to the left and right edges of the appliquéd background fabric. Sew a C square to each end of the horizontal borders. Press the seam allowances in the directions indicated by the arrows.

4. Sew the horizontal borders to the top and bottom edges of the appliquéd background fabric. Press the seam allowances in the directions indicated by the arrows.

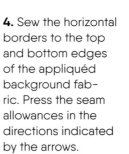

5. Layer the pillow top, batting and muslin base. Baste (refer to page 43).

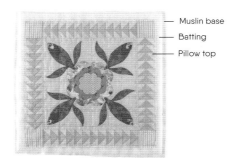

- Muslin base
- Batting
- Pillow top

6. Quilt as shown in the diagram on page 71. Baste to mark the finishing lines. Trim the excess batting and muslin to match the size of the pillow top.

7. Make the pillow back: Adhere the strips of fusible interfacing to the opening edge on each back piece. Fold each opening edge over to the wrong side ¼ in (7 mm) and topstitch.

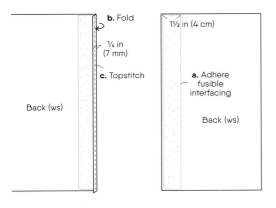

b. Fold

¼ in (7 mm)

c. Topstitch

Back (ws)

1½ in (4 cm)

a. Adhere fusible interfacing

Back (ws)

8. Make the buttonholes on one back piece and sew the buttons to the other, following the placement indicated in the diagram on page 71.

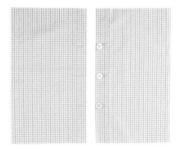

9. Button the two back pieces together. Baste a short seam along the top and bottom to hold the two pieces together, then unbutton.

10. Align the pillow front and back with right sides together. Sew around all four edges.

11. Turn right side out. Hand stitch the lace to the seam. Sew the buttons to the lace. Insert a pillow form.

BRODERIE PERSE TECHNIQUES

Broderie perse allows you to create your own fabrics by fussy cutting specific motifs and appliquéing them to another piece of fabric. The following guide explains how to select fabrics for broderie perse, how to fussy cut motifs, and how to appliqué them to a background fabric.

A Note on Selecting Fabric

When selecting fabric for broderie perse, look for motifs with clearly outlined shapes that can be fussy cut easily. When collecting fabric for your stash, remember to incorporate prints of various sizes.

How to Cut Fabric for Broderie Perse

1. On the right side of the fabric, use a pencil to lightly outline the motif about ⅛ in (3 mm) from the print. This will be the finishing line, so do your best to follow the shape of the fabric print.

Note: Take care not to make your lines too angular or your curves too rounded. You want to trace the shape as accurately as possible.

2. Cut out the motif, leaving ⅛ in (3 mm) seam allowance from the marked line.

How to Sew Broderie Perse

1. Baste the motif to the background fabric. If you're using a small motif, you can glue the motif in place.

2. Next, you will buttonhole stitch the motif to the background fabric (see below).

3. Buttonhole stitch around the entire motif, working from left to right.

Points

Make three stitches starting from the same hole on the motif.

Curves

Make two stitches ending in the same hole on the background fabric.

V-Shapes

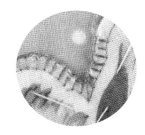

Make three stitches ending in the same hole on the background fabric.

HOW TO BUTTONHOLE STITCH

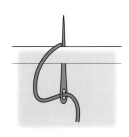

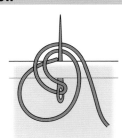

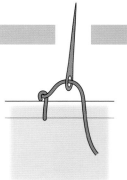

4. Make another stitch about 1/16 in (2 mm) away.

1. Starting from the wrong side, insert the needle through the background fabric and draw it out right on the edge of the appliqué. Insert the needle through both layers along the finishing line. Bring the needle back up to the right side through the same hole.

2. Position the thread loop beneath the needle tip.

3. Pull the needle to tighten the loop.

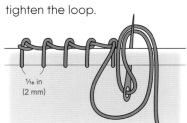

1/16 in (2 mm)

5. Continue making buttonhole stitches to attach the appliqué to the background fabric.

THE PATCHWORK POUCH

Shown on page 8

Materials

- **Patchwork fabric:** 11 assorted prints
- **Lining fabric:** One fat eighth
- One fat eighth of muslin

- **Batting:** 9½ x 14¼ in (24 x 36 cm)
- One ⅝ in (1.5 cm) magnetic snap
- 19¾ in (50 cm) of ⅝ in (1.5 cm) wide ribbon

Sew using ¼ in (7 mm) seam allowance, unless otherwise noted.

Project Diagram

Diagrams show finished measurements (seam allowance not included).

Pouch

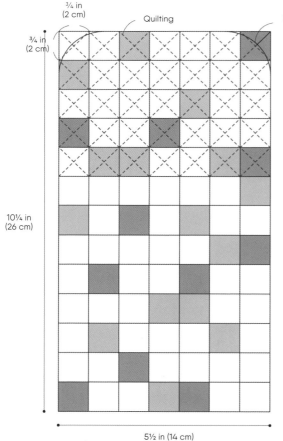

¾ in (2 cm)

¾ in (2 cm)

Quilting

Use template to round corners

10¼ in (26 cm)

5½ in (14 cm)

Cutting Instructions

Trace and cut out the template on Pattern Sheet A. Cut out the following pieces, adding ¼ in (7 mm) seam allowance.

Lining fabric

- 1 lining

Cut out the following fabric pieces, which do not have templates, according to the measurements below (these measurements include seam allowance).

Patchwork fabric

- Squares (cut 91): 1¼ in (3.4 cm) each

Batting

- Pouch batting: 9½ x 14¼ in (24 x 36 cm)

Muslin

- Pouch muslin base: 9½ x 14¼ in (24 x 36 cm)

Construction Steps

1. Make the top: Sew 91 squares together in 13 rows of seven, as shown in the diagram on page 76.

2. Layer the top, batting, and muslin base. Quilt as shown in the diagram on page 76. Trim the excess batting and muslin to match the size of the top. Align the top and lining with right sides together. Use the template on Pattern Sheet A to mark the stitching lines, including the rounded upper corners. Sew the lining to the top, leaving a 4 in (10 cm) opening along one side. Trim the excess fabric and batting at the corners, leaving ¼ in (7 mm) seam allowance..

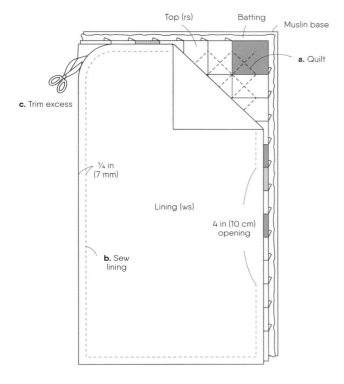

Top (rs) Batting Muslin base
a. Quilt
c. Trim excess
¼ in (7 mm)
Lining (ws)
4 in (10 cm) opening
b. Sew lining

3. Turn the pouch right side out and hand stitch the opening closed.

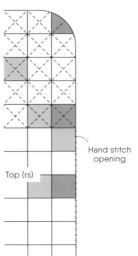

Hand stitch opening
Top (rs)

4. Fold the bottom of the pouch up along the line marked on the template. Hand stitch the fold in place along the left and right edges of the pouch, making your stitches through the linings. Sew the magnetic snap components to the pouch, following the placement noted in the diagram below.

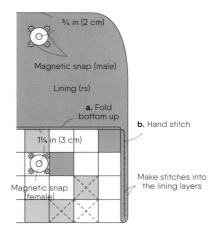

¾ in (2 cm)
Magnetic snap (male)
Lining (rs)
a. Fold bottom up
b. Hand stitch
1¼ in (3 cm)
Make stitches into the lining layers
Magnetic snap (female)

5. Tie the ribbon into a bow. Slipstitch the bow to the flap on the pouch outside.

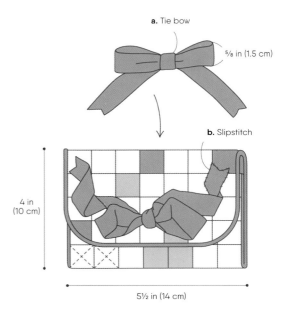

a. Tie bow
⅝ in (1.5 cm)
b. Slipstitch
4 in (10 cm)
5½ in (14 cm)

SQUARE ZIP CASE

Shown on page 9

Materials

- **Patchwork fabric:** Eight assorted prints (8 in [20 cm] square of each)
- **Back fabric:** One fat eighth of large floral print
- **Lining fabric:** One fat quarter
- One fat quarter of muslin
- **Batting:** 13½ x 15¾ in (34 x 40 cm)

- **Binding fabric:** 15¾ in (40 cm) square of linen
- 1 yd (0.9 m) of ⅛ in (3 mm) diameter cord
- One 9 in (23 cm) zipper
- One fur pompom
- Linen thread

Sew using ¼ in (7 mm) seam allowance, unless otherwise noted.

Project Diagram

Diagrams show finished measurements (seam allowance not included).

Front

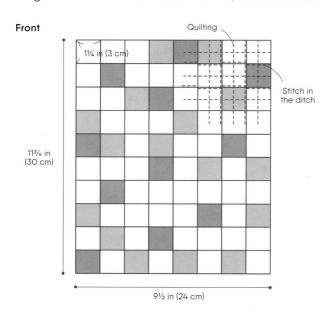

Quilting

1¼ in (3 cm)

Stitch in the ditch

11¾ in (30 cm)

9½ in (24 cm)

Back

11¾ in (30 cm)

9½ in (24 cm)

Cutting Instructions

Cut out the following fabric pieces, which do not have templates, according to the measurements below (these measurements include seam allowance).

Patchwork fabric
- Squares (cut 80): 1¾ in (4.4 cm) each

Batting:
- Case batting: 13½ x 15¾ in (34 x 40 cm)

Muslin
- Case muslin base: 13½ x 15¾ in (34 x 40 cm)

Back fabric
- Case back: 10 x 12¼ in (25.4 x 31.4 cm)

Binding fabric
- Binding: 24¾ in (63 cm) of 1¼ in (3 cm) wide single-fold bias binding

Lining fabric
- Case linings (cut 2): 10 x 12¼ in (25.4 x 31.4 cm)

Construction Steps

1. Make the front: Sew 80 squares together in 10 rows of eight, as shown in the diagram on page 78.

2. Layer the front, batting, and muslin base. Quilt as shown in the diagram on page 78. Trim the excess batting and muslin to match the size of the front. Align the front and back with right sides together. Sew, leaving the top open. Turn right side out.

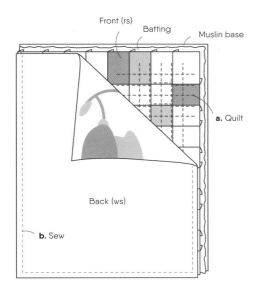

3. Hand stitch the cord to the seams (refer to step 5 diagram for placement).

4. Make the lining: Sew the two lining pieces with right sides together, leaving the top open. Insert the lining into the case with wrong sides together. Baste together around the top opening.

5. Bind the opening: With right sides together, sew the short ends of the binding to form a loop matching the size of the opening. With right sides together, sew the binding loop to the case. Wrap the binding around the seam allowances and hand stitch to the lining.

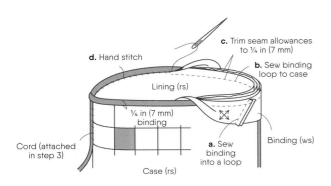

6. Hand stitch the zipper to the binding on the inside of the case. The stitches should not be visible on the outside of the case.

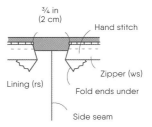

7. Attach the fur pompom to the zipper pull to complete the case.

How to Attach the Pompom

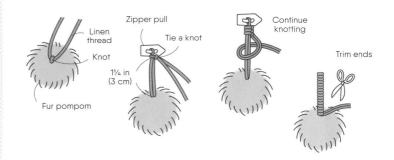

Finished Diagram

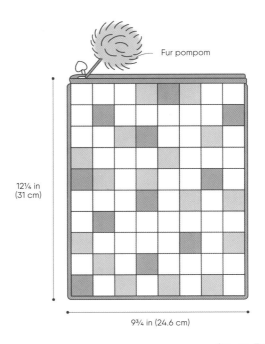

NINE PATCH TOTE

Shown on page 10

Materials

- **Patchwork fabric:** Five print fat eighths
- **Main fabric:** 1 yd (1 m) of linen
- **Lining/pocket fabric:** ¾ yd (0.7 m)
- ¾ yd (0.7 m) of muslin
- **Batting:** 21¾ x 29¼ in (55 x 74 cm)

- **Fusible interfacing:** 18¼ x 25¾ in (46.4 x 65.4 cm)
- 16 in (40.5 cm) leather handles
- Two leather tabs with D-rings
- One 16 in (40 cm) zipper
- One 7 in (18 cm) braided leather zipper pull

Sew using ¼ in (7 mm) seam allowance, unless otherwise noted.

Project Diagram

Diagrams show finished measurements (seam allowance not included).

Bag Outside

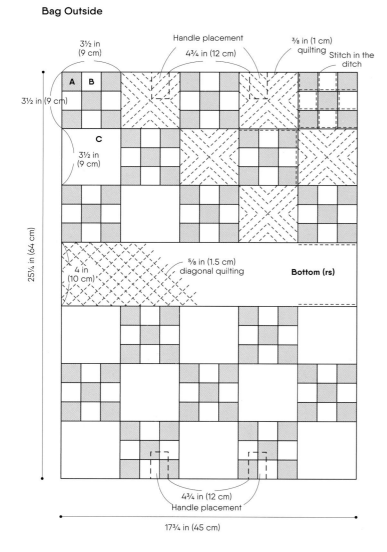

Lining (make 2)

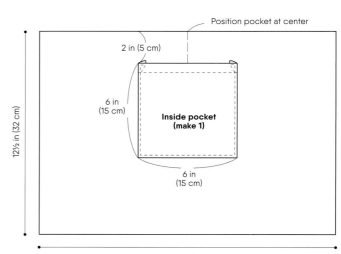

Cutting Instructions

Cut out the following fabric pieces, which do not have templates, according to the measurements below (these measurements include ¼ in [7 mm] seam allowance).

Patchwork fabric

- A squares (cut 75): 1¾ in (4.4 cm) each

Main fabric

- B squares (cut 60): 1¾ in (4.4 cm) each
- C squares (cut 15): 4 in (10.4 cm) each
- Bottom: 4½ x 18¼ in (11.4 x 46.4 cm)

Batting

- Bag batting: 21¾ x 29¼ in (55 x 74 cm)

Muslin

- Bag muslin base: 21¾ x 29¼ in (55 x 74 cm)

Fusible interfacing

- Bag interfacing: 18¼ x 25¾ in (46.4 x 65.4 cm)

Main fabric

- Binding: 1¼ yds (1.2 m) of 1¼ in (3 cm) wide single-fold bias binding

Lining fabric

- Bag linings (cut 2): 13 x 18¼ in (33.4 x 46.4 cm)
- Inside pocket: 6½ x 7 ⅛ in (16.4 x 17.9 cm)

Construction Steps

1. Make the nine patches: Sew five A squares and four B squares together to make each nine patch block. Make 15 nine patch blocks total.

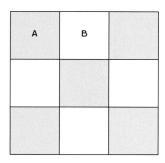

Make 15 blocks

2. Make the bag top: Alternately sew the nine patch blocks and C squares together to make the two patchwork sections. Note that one section will have eight nine patches and the other will have seven. Sew the bottom to each patchwork section.

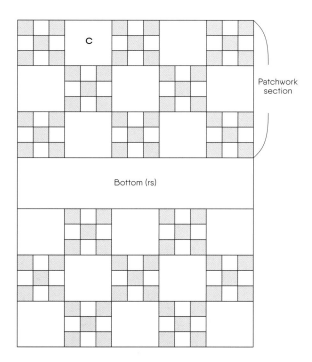

Patchwork section

Bottom (rs)

3. Layer the bag top, batting and muslin base. Quilt as shown in the diagram on page 80. Trim the excess batting and muslin to match the size of the top. Adhere fusible interfacing to the muslin base.

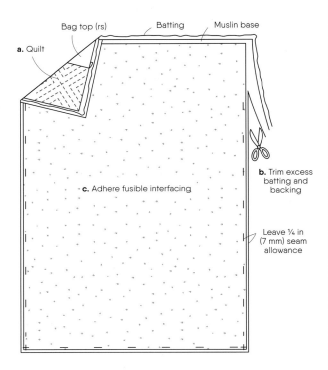

a. Quilt

Bag top (rs) Batting Muslin base

c. Adhere fusible interfacing

b. Trim excess batting and backing

Leave ¼ in (7 mm) seam allowance

> **Note:** This bag is constructed with batting, a muslin base and a layer of fusible interfacing to provide support and structure. A separate lining will be added to hide these layers. You could also use a foam interfacing instead and skip these steps.

4. Fold the bag in half with right sides together. Sew together along the sides.

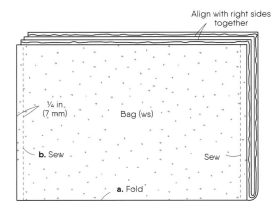

Align with right sides together

¼ in. (7 mm)

Bag (ws)

b. Sew

Sew

a. Fold

5. Miter each corner as shown below.

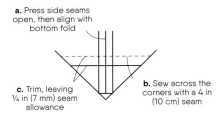

a. Press side seams open, then align with bottom fold

c. Trim, leaving ¼ in (7 mm) seam allowance

b. Sew across the corners with a 4 in (10 cm) seam

6. Make the inside pocket and topstitch to the lining.

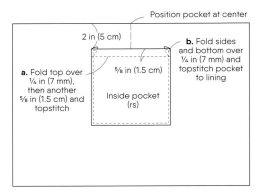

Position pocket at center

2 in (5 cm)

b. Fold sides and bottom over ¼ in (7 mm) and topstitch pocket to lining

a. Fold top over ¼ in (7 mm), then another ⅝ in (1.5 cm) and topstitch

⅝ in (1.5 cm)

Inside pocket (rs)

7. Sew the two lining pieces with right sides together, leaving the top open. Use the same process shown in step 5 to miter the lining corners.

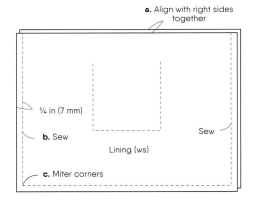

a. Align with right sides together

¼ in (7 mm)

b. Sew

Sew

Lining (ws)

c. Miter corners

8. Insert the lining into the bag with wrong sides together. Baste together around the bag opening.

9. Bind the bag opening: With right sides together, sew the short ends of the binding to form a loop matching the size of the bag opening. With right sides together, sew the binding loop to the bag. Wrap the binding around the seam allowances and hand stitch to the lining.

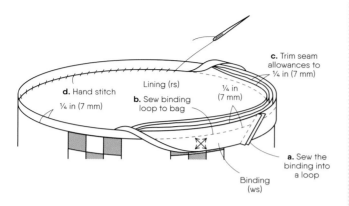

c. Trim seam allowances to ¼ in (7 mm)

Lining (rs)

d. Hand stitch ¼ in (7 mm)

b. Sew binding loop to bag

¼ in (7 mm)

a. Sew the binding into a loop

Binding (ws)

10. Hand stitch the zipper to the binding on the inside of the bag. The stitches should not be visible on the outside of the bag.

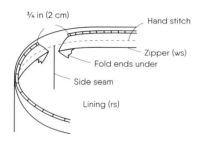

¾ in (2 cm)

Hand stitch

Zipper (ws)

Fold ends under

Side seam

Lining (rs)

11. Backstitch the handles to the bag, following the placement noted in the diagram below. Take care not to stitch through the lining.

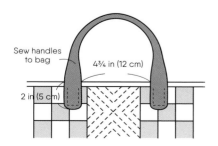

Sew handles to bag

4¾ in (12 cm)

2 in (5 cm)

12. Backstitch the tabs to the bag side seams. Take care not to stitch through the lining.

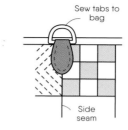

Sew tabs to bag

Side seam

13. Attach the zipper charm to complete the bag.

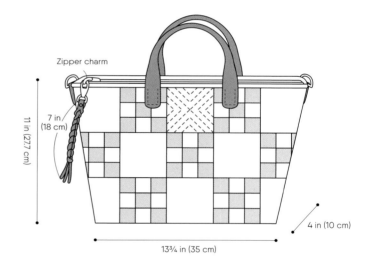

Zipper charm

11 in (27.7 cm)

7 in (18 cm)

4 in (10 cm)

13¾ in (35 cm)

SPARKLING DIAMONDS QUILT

Shown on page 11

Materials

- **Main fabric:** 3½ yds (3.2 m) of off-white floral print
- **Patchwork fabric #1:** Eight assorted print scraps
- **Patchwork fabric #2:** ½ yd (0.5 m) of off-white solid
- **Backing/binding fabric:** 5 yds (4.6 m) of 43 in (109 cm) wide

or 2½ yds (2.3 m) of 108 in (275 cm) extra-wide floral print fabric

- **Batting:** 56¾ x 69½ in (144 x 176 cm)
- No. 25 embroidery floss in red

Project Diagram

Diagrams show finished measurements (seam allowance not included).

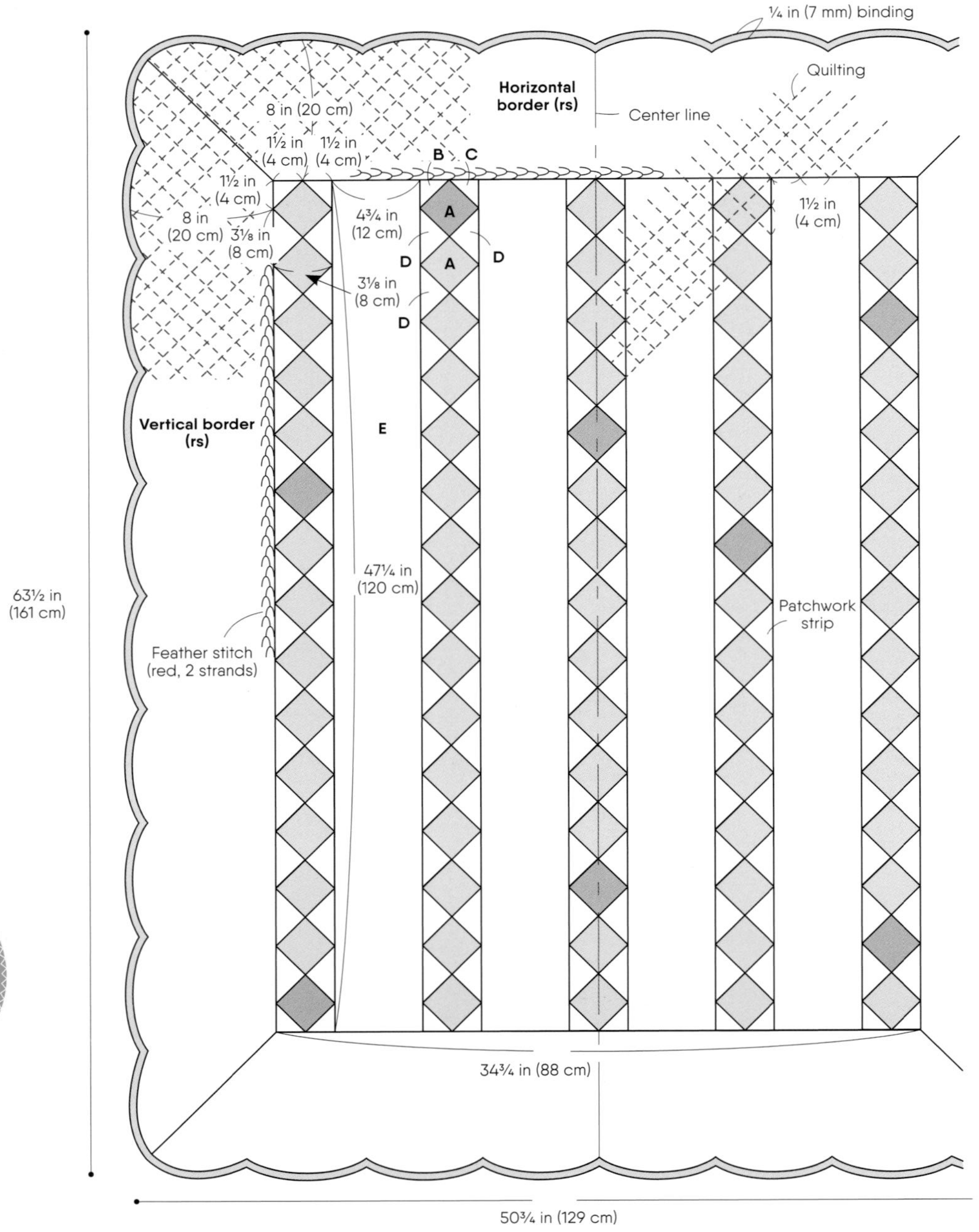

¼ in (7 mm) binding

Quilting

Horizontal border (rs)

Center line

8 in (20 cm)

1½ in (4 cm) 1½ in (4 cm)

B C

1½ in (4 cm)

4¾ in (12 cm)

A

1½ in (4 cm)

8 in (20 cm) 3⅛ in (8 cm)

D A D

3⅛ in (8 cm)

D

Vertical border (rs)

E

63½ in (161 cm)

47¼ in (120 cm)

Patchwork strip

Feather stitch (red, 2 strands)

Sew using ¼ in (7 mm) seam allowance, unless otherwise noted.

34¾ in (88 cm)

50¾ in (129 cm)

Cutting Instructions

Trace and cut out the templates on Pattern Sheet A. Cut out the following pieces, adding ¼ in (7 mm) seam allowance.

Patchwork fabric #2

- 10 B pieces
- 10 C pieces
- 140 D pieces

Cut out the following fabric pieces, which do not have templates, according to the measurements below (these measurements include ¼ in [7 mm] seam allowance).

Patchwork fabric #1

- A squares (cut 75): 2¾ in (7 cm) each

Main fabric

- E (cut 4) pieces: 5¼ x 53¾ in (13.4 x 136.4 cm)
- Horizontal borders (cut 2): 8½ x 56¾ in (21.4 x 144 cm)
- Vertical borders (cut 2): 8½ x 69¼ in (21.4 x 176 cm)

Backing/binding fabric

- Quilt backing: 56¾ x 69½ in (144 x 176 cm)
- Binding: 7¼ yds (6.5 m) of 1¼ in (3 cm) wide single-fold bias binding

Batting

- Quilt batting: 56¾ x 69½ in (144 x 176 cm)

Construction Steps

1. Sew pieces A–D together to make five patchwork strips, each with 15 A squares, as shown in the diagram on page 84.

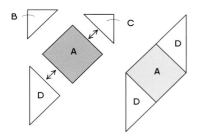

2. With right sides together, alternately sew the patchwork strips and E pieces together to complete the quilt top. Trim the E pieces to match the length of the patchwork strips. **Note:** The cutting dimensions for the E pieces include about 6 in (15 cm) extra length to accommodate for any variation with the finished patchwork strip length.

3. Sew the mitered borders to the quilt top (refer to page 51).

4. If desired, embroider along the border seams with the feather stitch.

5. Mark the quilting lines. Use the template on Pattern Sheet A to mark the scalloped finishing lines along the borders.

6. Layer the top, batting, and backing. Quilt as shown in the diagram on page 84.

7. Bind the quilt: With right sides together, sew the binding to the quilt top along the marked scalloped finishing lines. Trim the excess batting and backing fabric, leaving ¼ in (7 mm) seam allowance. Make clips into the seam allowance at the concave scallop curves. Take care not to clip through the stitching. Wrap the binding around the seam allowances and hand stitch to the backing.

Feather Stitch

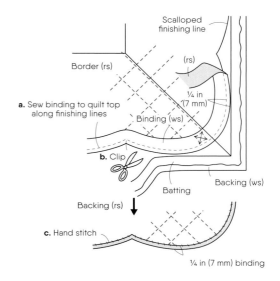

TIC TAC TOE PILLOW
Shown on page 11

Materials

- **Patchwork fabric #1:** Eight assorted print scraps
- **Patchwork fabric #2:** ⅝ yd (0.6 m) of off-white solid
- **Patchwork fabric #3:** One fat quarter of red floral print
- ⅝ yd (0.6 m) of muslin
- **Batting:** 19¾ in (50 cm) square

- **Fusible interfacing:** 4 x 19¾ in (10 x 50 cm)
- Three ¾ in (1.8 cm) diameter buttons
- 1½ yds (1.4 m) of ½ in (1.3 cm) wide lace
- 2 yds (1.8 m) of ½ in (1.3 cm) wide rickrack

> Sew using ¼ in (7 mm) seam allowance, unless otherwise noted.

Project Diagram

Diagrams show finished measurements (seam allowance not included).

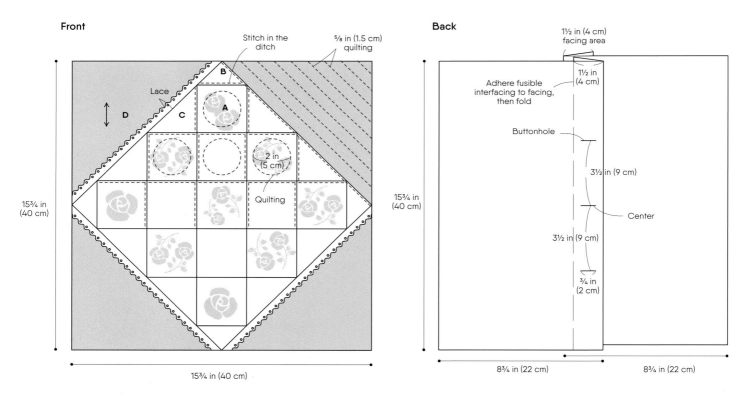

Front

Stitch in the ditch

⅝ in (1.5 cm) quilting

Lace

B

A

D

C

2 in (5 cm)

Quilting

15¾ in (40 cm)

15¾ in (40 cm)

Back

1½ in (4 cm) facing area

1½ in (4 cm)

Adhere fusible interfacing to facing, then fold

Buttonhole

3½ in (9 cm)

Center

3½ in (9 cm)

¾ in (2 cm)

15¾ in (40 cm)

8¾ in (22 cm)

8¾ in (22 cm)

Cutting Instructions

Trace and cut out the templates on Pattern Sheet A. Cut out the following fabric pieces, adding ¼ in (7 mm) seam allowance.

Patchwork fabric #1
- 9 A squares

Patchwork fabric #2
- 4 A squares
- 4 B pieces
- 8 C pieces

Patchwork fabric #3
- 4 D pieces

Cut out the following fabric pieces, which do not have templates, according to the measurements below (these measurements include seam allowance).

Batting
- Pillow batting: 19¾ in (50 cm) square

Muslin
- Pillow muslin base: 19¾ in (50 cm) square

Patchwork fabric #2
- Back pieces (cut 2): 10½ x 16¼ in (26.7 x 41.4 cm)

Fusible interfacing
- Facings (cut 2): 1½ x 16¼ in (4 x 41.4 cm)

Construction Steps

1. Sew pieces A–D together to make the pillow front, as shown in the diagram on page 86.

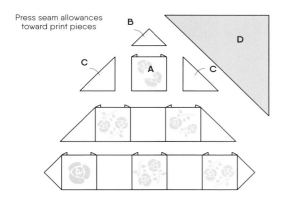

Press seam allowances toward print pieces

2. Layer the pillow front, batting, and muslin base. Quilt as shown in the diagram on page 86. **Note:** There is a quilting template for this project on Pattern Sheet A. Trim the excess batting and muslin to match the size of the pillow front.

3. Sew the lace to pillow front, following the placement noted in the diagram on page 86.

4. Adhere fusible interfacing to the facing area on the wrong side of each back piece. On each back piece, fold the facing under 1½ in (4 cm). Press, then stitch in place.

5. Make buttonholes on one back piece, following the placement noted in the diagram on page 86.

6. Overlap the facings on the two back pieces. Take care to align the back piece with the buttonholes on top of the other back piece. Baste together along the top and bottom to hold the overlapped areas in place.

7. To attach by machine, baste the rickrack to the seam allowance line on the right side of the pillow front. Align the pillow front and back with right sides together. Sew together around all four edges of the pillow.

8. Turn the pillow right side out. If attaching by hand, stitch the rickrack to the edges of the pillow. Sew the buttons to the back.

Finished Diagram

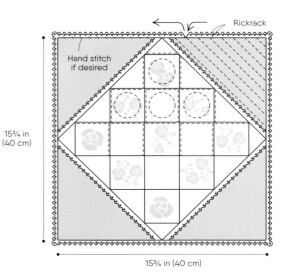

Rickrack

Hand stitch if desired

15¾ in (40 cm)

15¾ in (40 cm)

GARDEN TAPESTRY

Shown on page 13

Materials

- **Center fabric:** ¼ yd (0.25 m) of large floral print
- **Strip fabric:** 14 assorted fat quarters
- **Border/binding fabric:** 1¼ yds (1.25 m) of beige polka dot

- **Backing fabric:** 1¼ yds (1.25 m)
- **Batting:** 39½ x 39½ in (100 x 100 cm)
- 3 yds (2.8 m) of ¾ in (2 cm) wide lace

Sew using ¼ in (7 mm) seam allowance, unless otherwise noted.

Project Diagram

Diagrams show finished measurements (seam allowance not included).

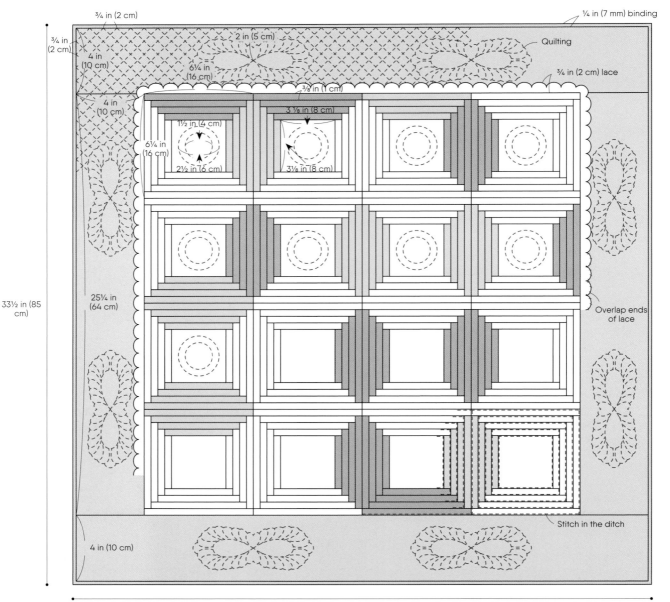

Cutting Instructions

Trace and cut out the templates on Pattern Sheet A. Cut out the following fabric pieces, adding ¼ in (7 mm) seam allowance.

Center fabric

- 16 centers

Strip fabric

- Strips for 16 blocks (refer to the photo on page 13 for fabric placement)

Cut out the following fabric pieces, which do not have templates, according to the measurements below (these measurements include seam allowance).

Border/binding fabric

- Vertical borders (cut 2): 4½ x 25¾ in (11.4 x 65.4 cm)
- Horizontal borders (cut 2): 4½ x 34 in (11.4 x 86.4 cm)
- Binding: 3¾ yds (3.4 m) of 1¼ in (3 cm) wide single-fold bias binding

Batting

- Quilt batting: 39½ in (100 cm) square

Backing fabric

- Quilt backing: 39½ in (100 cm) square

Construction Steps

1. Make 16 courthouse steps blocks as shown in the guide on page 54.

2. Make the quilt top: Sew the courthouse steps blocks into four rows of four, taking care to align like fabrics on adjacent blocks (refer to the photo on page 13).

3. Sew the vertical borders to the left and right edges of the quilt and the horizontal borders to the top and bottom edges.

4. Layer the top, batting, and backing. Quilt as shown in the diagram on page 88. **Note:** There are quilting templates for this project on Pattern Sheet A.

5. Bind the quilt (refer to page 45).

6. Appliqué the lace to the border seams.

LOG CABIN GUSSET BAG

Shown on page 14

Materials

- **Center fabric:** 4 in (10 cm) square of solid red
- **Strip fabric:** 12 assorted fat eighths in browns and reds
- **Main fabric:** ¾ yd (0.7 m) of large floral print
- **Lining fabric:** ½ yd (0.5 m)
- ½ yd (0.5 m) of muslin

- **Batting:** 19¾ x 43¼ in (50 x 110 cm)
- **Fusible interfacing:** 15¾ x 39½ in (40 x 110 cm)
- 55 in (140 cm) of ⅛ in (3 mm) diameter cord
- One set of 9¾ in (25 cm) handles

Sew using ¼ in (7 mm) seam allowance, unless otherwise noted.

Project Diagram

Diagrams show finished measurements (seam allowance not included).

Bag Outsides (make 2)

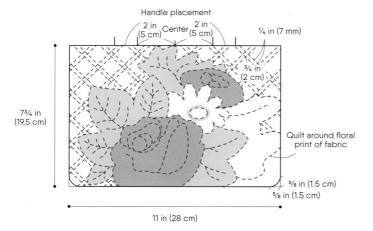

Lining (make 2)

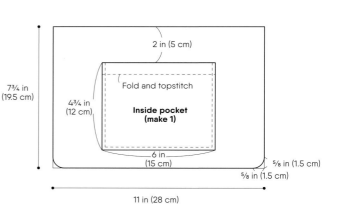

Gusset

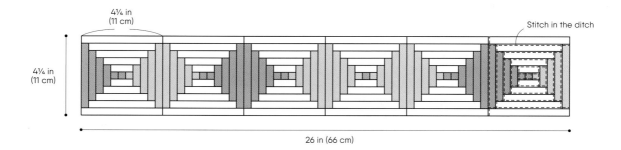

Cutting Instructions

Trace and cut out the templates on Pattern Sheet A. Cut out the following fabric pieces, adding ¼ in (7 mm) seam allowance.

Center fabric
- 6 centers

Strip fabric
- Strips for 6 blocks (refer to the photo on page 14 for fabric placement)

Cut out the following fabric pieces, which do not have templates, according to the measurements below (these measurements include seam allowance).

Main fabric
- Bag outsides (cut 2): 8¼ x 11½ in (20.9 x 29.4 cm)
- Binding: 1 yd (1 m) of 1¼ in (3 cm) wide single-fold bias binding

Batting
- Gusset batting: 8¼ x 30 in (21 x 76 cm)
- Bag battings (cut 2): 11¾ x 15 in (29.5 x 38 cm)

Muslin
- Gusset muslin base: 8¼ x 30 in (21 x 76 cm)
- Bag muslin bases (cut 2): 11¾ x 15 in (29.5 x 38 cm)

Lining fabric
- Inside pocket: 6 ⅛ x 6¾ in (15.5 x 17 cm)
- Bag linings (cut 2): 8¼ x 11½ in (20.9 x 29.4 cm)
- Gusset lining: 4¾ x 26½ in (12.4 x 67.4 cm)

Fusible interfacing
- Bag interfacings (cut 2): 8¼ x 11½ in (20.9 x 29.4 cm)
- Gusset interfacing: 4¾ x 26½ in (12.4 x 67.4 cm)

Construction Steps

1. Make six courthouse steps blocks as shown in the guide on page 54. Sew the six blocks together as shown in the diagram on page 90 to form the gusset.

2. Quilt the gusset: Layer the gusset, batting, and muslin base. Quilt as shown in the diagram on page 90. Trim the batting and muslin to match the size of the gusset. Adhere fusible interfacing to the muslin base.

> **Note:** This bag is constructed with batting, a muslin base, and a layer of fusible interfacing to provide support and structure. A separate lining will be added to hide these layers. You could also use a foam interfacing instead and skip these steps.

3. Make the bag outsides: Mark the quilting lines on each bag outside. Layer each bag outside, batting, and muslin base. Quilt as shown in the diagram on page 90. Trim the batting and muslin to match the size of the bag outsides. Adhere fusible interfacing to the muslin base.

4. Make the rounded corners: Mark each side ⅝ in (1.5 cm) from the bottom corners. Connect the marks with curved lines. Trim along the curves to round the bottom corners.

5. Sew the bag together: With right sides together, sew a long edge of the gusset to each bag outside.

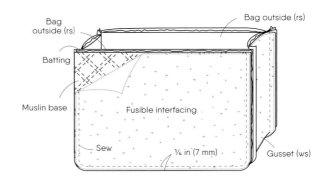

6. Turn the bag right side out. Hand stitch the cord to the gusset seams (refer to step 10 diagram for placement).

7. Make the inside pocket and topstitch to one lining piece, as shown below. On the lining pieces, mark each side ⅝ in (1.5 cm) from the bottom corners. Connect the marks with curved lines. Trim along the curves to round the bottom corners.

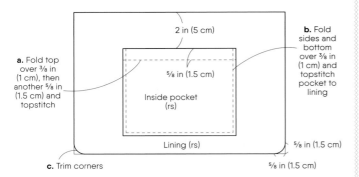

a. Fold top over ⅜ in (1 cm), then another ⅝ in (1.5 cm) and topstitch

2 in (5 cm)

b. Fold sides and bottom over ⅜ in (1 cm) and topstitch pocket to lining

⅝ in (1.5 cm)

Inside pocket (rs)

Lining (rs)

c. Trim corners

⅝ in (1.5 cm)

⅝ in (1.5 cm)

⅝ in (1.5 cm)

8. Make the lining: With right sides together, sew a long edge of the gusset lining to each bag lining. Insert the lining into the bag outside with wrong sides together. Baste together around the bag opening.

9. Align the wrong side of the handles with the lining so the handles are facing down (refer to the diagram on page 90 for handle placement). Sew the handles in place, taking care to stitch in the bag opening seam allowance. This will ensure that the raw edges of the handles are covered once the binding is attached.

10. Bind the opening: With right sides together, sew the short ends of the binding to form a loop matching the size of the opening. With right sides together, sew the binding loop to the bag. Wrap the binding around the seam allowances and hand stitch to the lining.

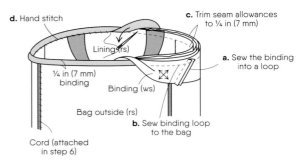

d. Hand stitch

c. Trim seam allowances to ¼ in (7 mm)

Lining (rs)

a. Sew the binding into a loop

¼ in (7 mm) binding

Binding (ws)

Bag outside (rs)

b. Sew binding loop to the bag

Cord (attached in step 6)

Finished Diagram

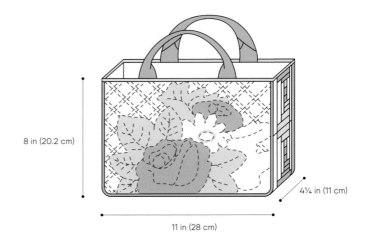

8 in (20.2 cm)

4¼ in (11 cm)

11 in (28 cm)

LOG CABIN FLOOR MAT

Shown on page 15

Materials

- **Main fabric:** ¾ yd (0.7 m) of large floral print
- **Block center fabric:** 6 x 8 in (15 x 20 cm) of solid red
- **Strip fabric:** Eight assorted taupe fat quarters

- **Backing fabric:** 1 yd (1 m)
- **Batting:** 31½ x 38½ in (79.4 x 97.4 cm)

Sew using ¼ in (7 mm) seam allowance, unless otherwise noted.

Project Diagram

Diagrams show finished measurements (seam allowance not included).

Cutting Instructions

Trace and cut out the templates on Pattern Sheet A. Cut out the following fabric pieces, adding ¼ in (7 mm) seam allowance.

Block center fabric

- 28 centers

Strip fabric

- Strips for 28 blocks (refer to the photo on page 15 for fabric placement)

Cut out the following fabric pieces, which do not have templates, according to the measurements below (these measurements include seam allowance).

Main fabric

- Mat center: 18¼ x 25¼ in (46.4 x 64.4 cm)
- Binding: 3½ yds (3.2 m) of 1¼ in (3 cm) wide single-fold bias binding

Batting

- Mat batting: 31½ x 38½ in (79.4 x 97.4 cm)

Backing fabric

- Mat backing: 31½ x 38½ in (79.4 x 97.4 cm)

Construction Steps

1. Make 28 courthouse steps blocks as shown in the guide on page 54.

2. Sew the blocks together in sets of seven to make four borders, taking care to align like fabrics on adjacent blocks (refer to the photo on page 15).

3. Sew two borders to the long edges of the mat center.

4. Sew the remaining two borders to the remaining edges of the mat center.

5. Layer the top, batting, and backing. Quilt as shown in the diagram on page 93. Trim the excess batting and backing to match the size of the top.

6. Bind the mat (refer to page 45).

COURTHOUSE STEPS TOTE

Shown on page 16

Materials

- **Patchwork fabric:** ¼ yd (0.25 m) of large floral print
- **Center fabric:** 4 x 8 in (10 x 20 cm) of brown checkered fabric
- **Strip fabric:** Seven assorted fat eighths in beiges and reds
- **Bottom/binding fabric:** ½ yd (0.5 m) of beige linen
- **Lining fabric:** ¾ yd (0.7 m)

- ¾ yd (0.7 m) of muslin
- **Batting:** 19¾ x 49¼ in (50 x 125 cm)
- **Fusible interfacing:** 17¾ x 39½ in (45 x 110 cm)
- 39½ in (100 cm) of ⅛ in (3 mm) diameter cord
- One set of 16¼ in (41 cm) leather handles
- 4¼ x 14½ in (11 x 37 cm) of plastic sheeting

Project Diagram

Diagrams show finished measurements (seam allowance not included).

Bag Outsides (make 1 of each)

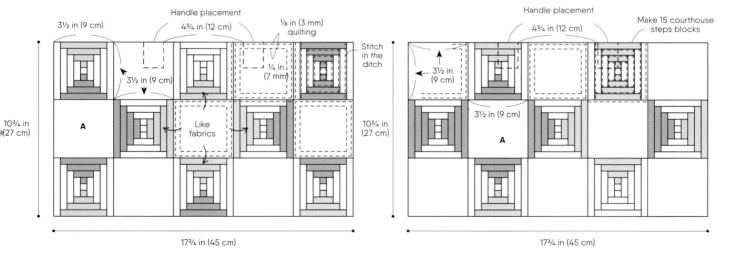

Bottom

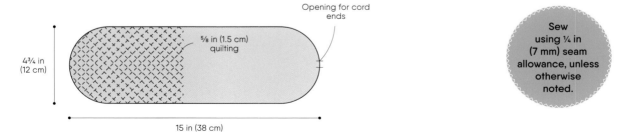

Sew using ¼ in (7 mm) seam allowance, unless otherwise noted.

Cutting Instructions

Trace and cut out the templates on Pattern Sheet A. Cut out the following fabric pieces, adding ¼ in (7 mm) seam allowance.

Center fabric
- 15 centers

Strip fabric
- Strips for 15 blocks (refer to the photo on page 16 for fabric placement)

Bottom/binding fabric
- 1 bottom

Batting
- 1 bottom*

Muslin
- 1 bottom muslin base*
- 1 bottom plate fabric (add ¾ in [2 cm] seam allowance to this piece)

Fusible interfacing
- 1 bottom

Plastic sheeting
- 1 bottom plate

Lining fabric
- 1 bottom

*Cut the bottom batting and muslin base out a few inches larger than the template on each side. They will be trimmed into shape once the layers have been quilted.

Cut out the following fabric pieces, which do not have templates, according to the measurements below (these measurements include seam allowance).

Patchwork fabric
- A (cut 15): 4 in (10.4 cm) squares

Batting
- Bag battings (cut 2): 14¾ x 21¾ in (37 x 55 cm)

Muslin
- Bag muslin bases (cut 2): 14¾ x 21¾ in (37 x 55 cm)

Bottom/binding fabric
- Binding: 1¼ yds (1.2 m) of 1¼ in (3 cm) wide single-fold bias binding

Fusible interfacing
- Bag interfacings (cut 2): 11 ¼ x 18 ¼ in (28.4 x 46.4 cm)

Lining fabric
- Linings (cut 2): 11¼ x 18¼ in (28.4 x 46.4 cm)

Construction Steps

1. Make 15 courthouse steps blocks as shown in the guide on page 54.

2. Make the bag outsides: Alternately sew the courthouse steps blocks and A squares together to make two bag outsides as shown in the diagram on page 95. Note that one bag outside will have eight courthouse steps blocks and the other will have seven courthouse steps blocks. Take care to align like fabrics on each side of the A squares (refer to the photo on page 16).

3. Layer each bag outside, batting, and muslin base. Quilt as shown in the diagram on page 95. Trim the excess batting and muslin to match the size of the bag outside. Adhere fusible interfacing to each muslin base.

Note: This bag is constructed with batting, a muslin base, and a layer of fusible interfacing to provide support and structure. A separate lining will be added to hide these layers. You could also use a foam interfacing instead and skip these steps.

4. Align the two bag outsides with right sides together. Sew together along the sides.

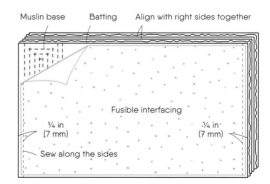

5. Make the bottom: Layer the bottom, batting, and muslin base. Quilt as shown in the diagram on page 95. Use the template on Pattern Sheet A to trim the bottom into shape, leaving ¼ in (7 mm) seam allowance. Adhere fusible interfacing to the muslin base.

6. Sew the bottom to the bag with right sides together, leaving a ³⁄₈ in (1 cm) opening at a side seam for the cord ends. Turn the bag right side out. Hand stitch the cord to the bottom seam. Insert the cord ends into the opening

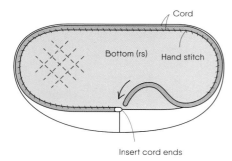

Cord

Bottom (rs)   Hand stitch

Insert cord ends

7. Sew the opening closed, stitching through the cords. Trim the excess cord.

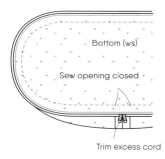

Bottom (ws)

Sew opening closed

Trim excess cord

8. Make the bottom plate as shown below, then hand stitch it in place on the inside of the bag.

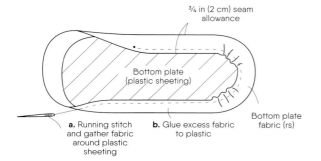

³⁄₄ in (2 cm) seam allowance

Bottom plate (plastic sheeting)

Bottom plate fabric (rs)

a. Running stitch and gather fabric around plastic sheeting

b. Glue excess fabric to plastic

9. Make the lining: Sew the two lining pieces with right sides together. Next, sew the bottom lining in place with right sides together. Insert the lining into the bag outside with wrong sides together. Baste together around the bag opening.

10. Bind the opening (refer to page 79): With right sides together, sew the short ends of the binding to form a loop matching the size of the opening. With right sides together, sew the binding loop to the bag. Wrap the binding around the seam allowances and hand stitch to the lining.

11. Backstitch the handles to the bag outside, following the placement noted in the diagram on page 95. Take care not to stitch through the lining.

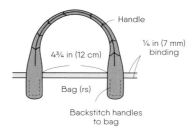

Handle

¼ in (7 mm) binding

4³⁄₄ in (12 cm)

Bag (rs)

Backstitch handles to bag

Finished Diagram

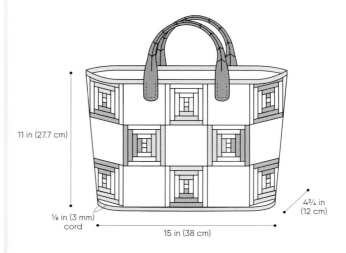

11 in (27.7 cm)

⅛ in (3 mm) cord

15 in (38 cm)

4³⁄₄ in (12 cm)

MARKET TOTE

Shown on page 17

Materials

- **Patchwork fabric:** 23 assorted scraps
- **Bottom/gusset fabric:** ½ yd (0.5 m) of large floral print
- **Binding fabric:** One fat quarter of solid brown
- **Lining fabric:** 1 yd (1 m)
- 1 yd (1 m) of muslin
- **Batting:** 31¾ x 35½ in (80 x 90 cm)

- **Fusible interfacing:** 27½ x 39½ in (70 x 100 cm)
- 45 in (114 cm) of ¾ in (2 cm) wide ribbon
- One set of 16 in (40.5 cm) webbing handles
- 9 x 12¼ in (23 x 31 cm) of plastic sheeting
- 59 in (150 cm) of ⅛ in (3 mm) diameter cord

Project Diagram

Diagrams show finished measurements (seam allowance not included).

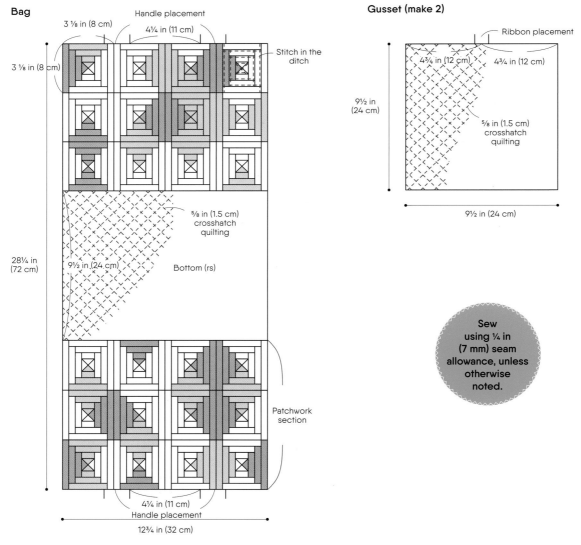

Bag

3 ⅛ in (8 cm)

Handle placement

4¼ in (11 cm)

3 ⅛ in (8 cm)

Stitch in the ditch

⅝ in (1.5 cm) crosshatch quilting

9½ in (24 cm)

Bottom (rs)

28¼ in (72 cm)

Patchwork section

4¼ in (11 cm)

Handle placement

12¾ in (32 cm)

Gusset (make 2)

Ribbon placement

4¾ in (12 cm)   4¾ in (12 cm)

9½ in (24 cm)

⅝ in (1.5 cm) crosshatch quilting

9½ in (24 cm)

Sew using ¼ in (7 mm) seam allowance, unless otherwise noted.

Cutting Instructions

Trace and cut out the templates on Pattern Sheet A. Cut out the following fabric pieces, adding ¼ in (7 mm) seam allowance.

Patchwork fabric

- 24 courthouse steps blocks, including hourglass square centers (refer to the photo on page 17 for fabric placement)

Cut out the following fabric pieces, which do not have templates, according to the measurements below (these measurements include seam allowance).

Bottom/gusset fabric

- Bottom: 10 x 13¼ in (25.4 x 33.4 cm)
- Gussets (cut 2): 10 in (25.4 cm) squares

Batting

- Bag batting: 16¾ x 32¼ in (42 x 82 cm)
- Gusset battings (cut 2): 13½ in (34 cm) squares

Muslin

- Bag muslin base: 16¾ x 32¼ in (42 x 82 cm)
- Gusset muslin bases (cut 2): 13½ in (34 cm) squares
- Bottom plate fabric: 10½ x 13¾ in (27 x 35 cm)

Fusible interfacing

- Bag interfacing: 13¼ x 28¾ in (33.4 x 73.4 cm)
- Gusset interfacings (cut 2): 10 in (25.4 cm) squares

Binding fabric

- Binding: 1½ yds (1.4 m) of 1¾ in (4.5 cm) wide single-fold bias binding

Lining fabric

- Bag lining: 13¼ x 28¾ in (33.4 x 73.4 cm)
- Gusset linings (cut 2): 10 in (25.4 cm) squares

Plastic sheeting

- Bottom plate: 9 x 12¼ in (23 x 31 cm)

Construction Steps

1. Make 24 courthouse steps blocks as shown in the guide on page 54. You will need to sew four triangles together to form each hourglass square center.

2. Make the bag top: Sew 12 courthouse steps blocks together to make each patchwork section, taking care to align like fabrics on adjacent blocks (refer to photo on page 17). Sew the bottom to the patchwork sections.

3. Layer the bag top, batting, and muslin base. Quilt as shown in the diagram on page 98. Trim the batting and muslin to match the size of the top. Adhere fusible interfacing to the muslin base.

Note: This bag is constructed with batting, a muslin base, and a layer of fusible interfacing to provide support and structure. A separate lining will be added to hide these layers. You could also use a foam interfacing instead and skip these steps.

4. Make the gussets: Layer each gusset, batting, and muslin base. Quilt as shown in the diagram on page 98. Trim the battings and muslin to match the size of the gussets. Adhere fusible interfacing to each muslin base.

5. Sew the bag together: With right sides together, sew the gussets to the bag following the numerical order shown in the diagram below. Make small clips into the seam allowance at the bottom corners. This will help the bag fold into shape.

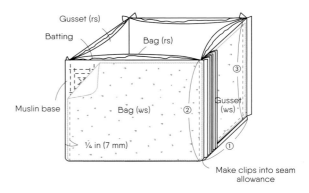

6. Turn the bag right side out. Hand stitch the cord to the gusset seams (refer to step 10 diagram for placement).

7. Make the bottom plate as shown below, then hand stitch it in place on the inside of the bag.

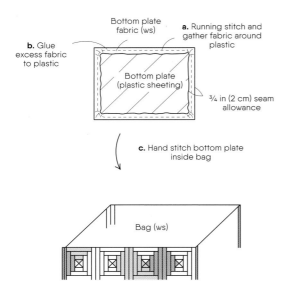

b. Glue excess fabric to plastic

Bottom plate fabric (ws)

a. Running stitch and gather fabric around plastic

Bottom plate (plastic sheeting)

¾ in (2 cm) seam allowance

c. Hand stitch bottom plate inside bag

Bag (ws)

8. Make the lining: Follow the same process used in step 5 to sew the gusset linings to the bag lining. Insert the lining into the bag with wrong sides together. Baste together around the bag opening.

9. Align the wrong side of the handles with the lining so the handles are facing down (refer to the diagram on page 98 for handle placement). Sew the handles in place, taking care to stitch in the bag opening seam allowance. This will ensure that the raw edges of the handles are covered once the binding is attached.

10. Bind the opening: With right sides together, sew the short ends of the binding to form a loop matching the size of the opening. With right sides together, sew the binding loop to the bag. Wrap the binding around the seam allowances and hand stitch to the lining.

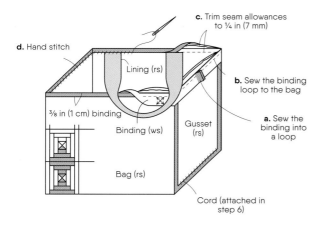

d. Hand stitch

c. Trim seam allowances to ¼ in (7 mm)

Lining (rs)

b. Sew the binding loop to the bag

⅜ in (1 cm) binding

Binding (ws)

Gusset (rs)

a. Sew the binding into a loop

Bag (rs)

Cord (attached in step 6)

11. Cut the ribbon into two 22½ in (57 cm) long pieces. On each piece, fold one short end under ⅜ in (1 cm) and topstitch. Fold the other short ends under ⅜ in (1 cm) and sew to the bag lining at the center of each gusset.

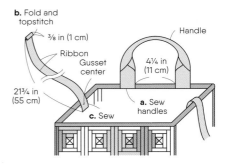

b. Fold and topstitch

⅜ in (1 cm)

Ribbon

Gusset center

Handle

4¼ in (11 cm)

21¾ in (55 cm)

c. Sew

a. Sew handles

Finished Diagram

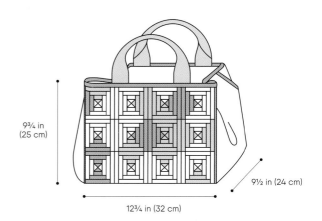

9¾ in (25 cm)

9½ in (24 cm)

12¾ in (32 cm)

BLOOMING HEXIES MINI QUILT

Shown on page 20

Materials

- **Main fabric:** One fat quarter of beige solid
- **Hexagon fabric:** 16 assorted red print scraps
- **Border fabric:** One fat quarter of floral print
- **Backing fabric:** One fat quarter

- **Batting:** 17¾ in (45 cm) square
- (123) ⅜ in (1 cm) hexagon precut EPP shapes
- 13¾ in (35 cm) square frame

Project Diagram

Diagrams show finished measurements (seam allowance not included).

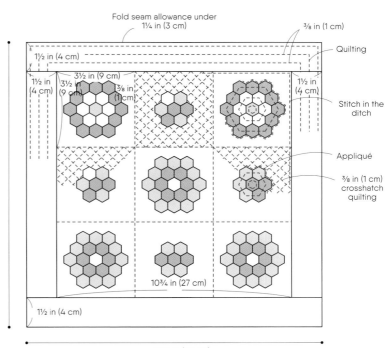

Sew using ¼ in (7 mm) seam allowance, unless otherwise noted.

Cutting Instructions

Trace and cut out the template on page 102. Cut out the following fabric pieces, adding ¼ in (7 mm) seam allowance.

Hexagon fabric

- 123 hexagons

Cut out the following fabric pieces, which do not have templates, according to the measurements below (these measurements include seam allowance).

Main fabric

- Main fabric: 11¼ in (28.4 cm) square

Border fabric

- Vertical borders (cut 2): 3 x 11¼ in (7.7 x 28.4 cm)
- Horizontal borders (cut 2): 3 x 16¼ in (7.7 x 41 cm)

Batting

- Batting: 17¾ in (45 cm) square

Backing fabric

- Backing: 17¾ in (45 cm) square

Construction Steps

1. Make 123 hexies as shown in the guide on page 55.

2. Sew the hexies together to make five large flowers and four small flowers (refer to page 57).

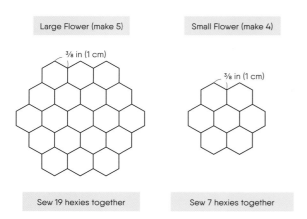

3. Appliqué the flowers to the main fabric, following the placement noted in the diagram on page 101.

4. With right sides together, sew the vertical borders to the left and right edges.

5. With right sides together, sew the horizontal borders to the top and bottom edges.

6. Layer the quilt top, batting, and backing. Quilt as shown in the diagram on page 101. Trim the excess batting and backing to match the size of the quilt top.

7. Fold and press the edges of the quilt over 1¼ in (3 cm) to the wrong side. Fold the quilt around the frame backing and tape to secure. Insert into the frame.

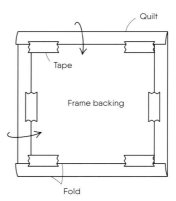

Note: You can also bind the quilt to make it a mini tapestry. You'll need about 1¾ yds (1.6 m) of binding. You'll want to cut the borders out 2 in (5.4 cm) wide instead of 3 in (7.7 cm) wide.

Full-Size Template

Note: This template should be used for piecing the hexies. Add ¼ in (7 mm) seam allowance to cut out each hexie.

APPLIQUÉD HEXIE POUCH

Shown on page 20

Materials

- **Hexagon fabric:** Three assorted print scraps
- **Broderie perse fabric:** Novelty print fabric scraps
- **Pouch fabric:** One fat quarter of metallic linen
- **Lining fabric:** One fat quarter
- One fat quarter of muslin
- **Batting:** 15¾ x 19¾ in (40 x 50 cm)

- One 7 in (18 cm) zipper
- 15¾ in (40 cm) of metallic rickrack
- Seven rhinestones
- No. 25 embroidery floss in gray
- (19) ⅜ in (1 cm) hexagon precut EPP shapes

> Sew using ¼ in (7 mm) seam allowance, unless otherwise noted.

Project Diagram

Diagrams show finished measurements (seam allowance not included).

Pouch Front

Broderie perse
Appliqué
Stitch in the ditch
7 in (18 cm)
⅜ in (1 cm)
⅛ in (3 mm)
4 in (10 cm)
8 in (20.5 cm)

Pouch Back

7 in (18 cm)
⅜ in (1 cm) crosshatch quilting
4 in (10 cm)
8 in (20.5 cm)

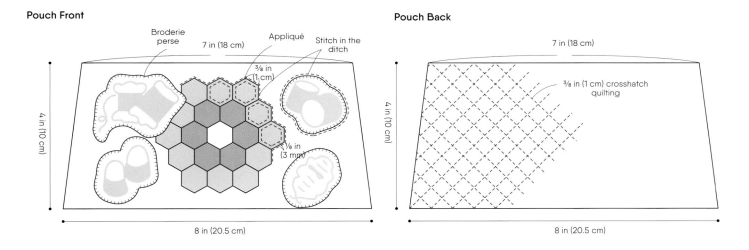

Bottom

⅜ in (1 cm) quilting
3¼ in (8.2 cm)
Cut on the bias
7 in (18 cm)

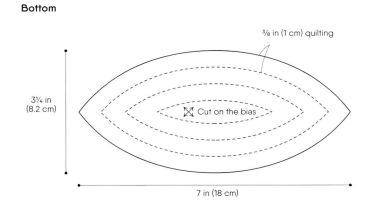

Cutting Instructions

For the broderie perse, fussy cut four novelty print motifs from the broderie perse fabric following the instructions on page 74. Trace and cut out the templates on page 105 and Pattern Sheet B. Cut out the following fabric pieces, adding ¼ in (7 mm) seam allowance.

Hexagon fabric

- 1 hexagon from fabric #1
- 6 hexagons from fabric #2
- 12 hexagons from fabric #3

Pouch fabric

- 2 pouch pieces
- 1 bottom (cut on the bias)

Batting

- 2 pouch pieces*
- 1 bottom*

Muslin

- 2 pouch muslin bases*
- 1 bottom muslin base*

Lining fabric

- 2 pouch pieces
- 1 bottom

*Cut the battings and muslin bases out a few inches larger than the template on each side. They will be trimmed into shape once the layers have been quilted.

Cut out the following fabric pieces, which do not have templates, according to the measurements below (these measurements include seam allowance).

Pouch fabric

- Binding: 20 in (51 cm) of 1¼ in (3 cm) wide single-fold bias binding

Construction Steps

1. Make 19 hexies and sew them into a flower as shown in the guide on page 55.

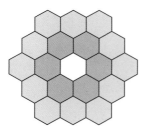

2. Appliqué the hexie flower to the center of the pouch front. Use the broderie perse technique shown on page 75 to embellish the pouch front with more appliqués.

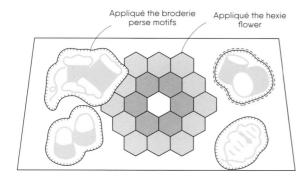

Appliqué the broderie perse motifs

Appliqué the hexie flower

3. Layer the pouch front, batting, and muslin base. Quilt as shown in the diagram on page 103. Trim the batting and muslin to match the size of the pouch front.

4. Use the same process to quilt and trim the pouch back and bottom into shape.

5. Align the pouch front and back with right sides together. Sew together along the sides.

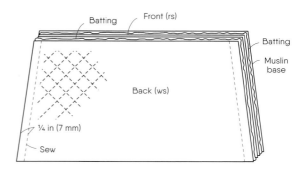

Batting

Front (rs)

Batting

Muslin base

Back (ws)

¼ in (7 mm)

Sew

6. Sew the bottom to pouch with right sides together.

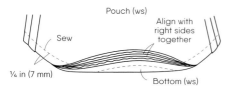

7. Make the lining: Sew the two lining pieces with right sides together. Next, sew the bottom lining in place with right sides together. Insert the lining into the pouch with wrong sides together. Baste together around the pouch opening.

8. Bind the opening: With right sides together, sew the short ends of the binding to form a loop matching the size of the opening. With right sides together, sew the binding loop to the pouch. Wrap the binding around the seam allowances and hand stitch to the lining.

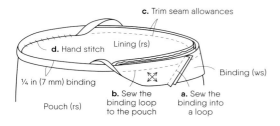

9. Hand stitch the zipper to the binding on the inside of the pouch. The stitches should not be visible on the outside of the pouch.

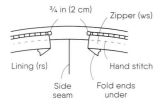

10. Hand stitch the rickrack to the pouch, covering the binding seam. Glue the rhinestones to the pouch front.

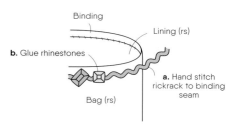

Finished Diagram

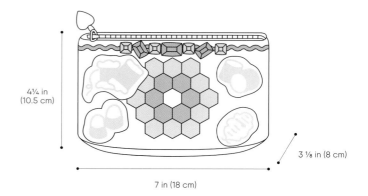

Full-Size Template

Note: This template should be used for piecing the hexies. Add ¼ in (7 mm) seam allowance to cut out each hexie.

HEXIES & STRIPES TAPESTRY

Shown on page 21

Materials

- **Hexagon fabric:** 15 assorted print scraps
- **Background fabric:** ¼ yd (0.25 m) of green print
- **Striped fabric:** ½ yd (0.5 m) of border print
- **Backing fabric:** 1 yd (1 m)
- **Binding fabric:** ⅝ yd (0.6 m) of green print

- **Batting:** 28 x 29¾ in (71 x 75 cm)
- (126) ½ in (1.2 cm) hexagon precut EPP shapes

Sew using ¼ in (7 mm) seam allowance, unless otherwise noted.

Project Diagram

Diagrams show finished measurements (seam allowance not included).

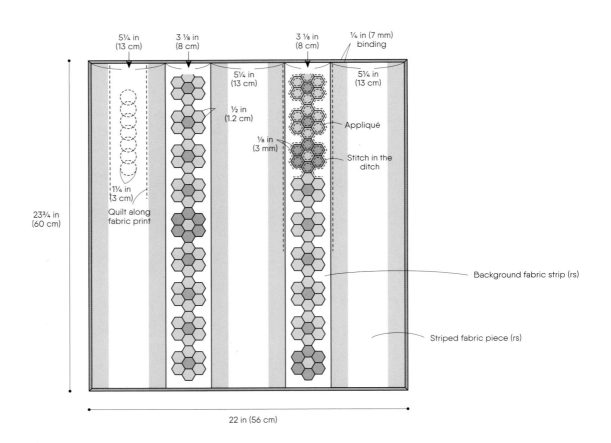

Cutting Instructions

Trace and cut out the template below. Cut out the following fabric pieces, adding ¼ in (7 mm) seam allowance.

Hexagon fabric

- 126 hexagons

Cut out the following fabric pieces, which do not have templates, according to the measurements below (these measurements include seam allowance).

Background fabric

- Background fabric strips (cut 2): 3 ⅝ x 23¾ in (9.4 x 60 cm)

Striped fabric

- Striped fabric pieces (cut 3): 5¾ x 23¾ in (14.4 x 60 cm)

Batting

- Batting: 28 x 29¾ in (71 x 75 cm)

Backing fabric

- Backing: 28 x 29¾ in (71 x 75 cm)

Binding fabric

- Binding: 2¾ yds (2.5 m) of 1¼ in (3 cm) wide single-fold bias binding

Construction Steps

1. Make 126 hexies as shown in the guide on page 55.

2. Sew the hexies together to make 18 flowers (refer to page 57).

Make 18

½ in (1.2 cm)

3. Sew the flowers together into two columns of nine flowers each.

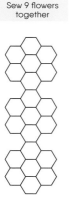

Sew 9 flowers together

4. Appliqué each column to a strip of background fabric.

5. With right sides together, alternately sew the striped fabric pieces and the appliquéd columns together to complete the quilt top.

6. Layer the quilt top, batting, and backing. Quilt as shown in the diagram on page 106. Trim the excess batting and backing to match the size of the quilt top.

7. Bind the quilt (refer to page 45).

Full-Size Template

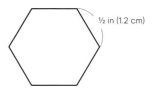

½ in (1.2 cm)

Note: This template should be used for piecing the hexies. Add ¼ in (7 mm) seam allowance to cut out each hexie.

HEXIE POCKET MINI TOTE

Shown on page 22

Materials

- **Hexagon fabric:** 30 assorted print scraps
- **Bag fabric:** One fat quarter of large floral print
- **Lining fabric:** One fat quarter
- **Binding fabric:** ½ yd (0.5 m) of red solid
- ⅝ yd (0.6 m) of muslin

- **Batting:** 21 x 36 in (53.5 x 91.5 cm)
- **Fusible interfacing:** 11¾ x 15¾ in (30 x 40 cm)
- One set of 10¾ in (27 cm) handles
- (166) ½ in (1.2 cm) hexagon precut EPP shapes

Sew using ¼ in (7 mm) seam allowance, unless otherwise noted.

Project Diagram

Diagrams show finished measurements (seam allowance not included).

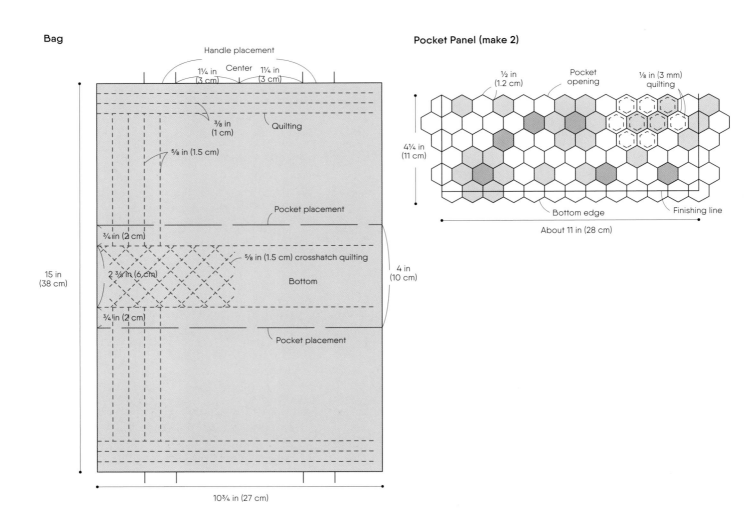

Bag

Handle placement

1¼ in (3 cm) Center 1¼ in (3 cm)

⅜ in (1 cm)

Quilting

⅝ in (1.5 cm)

Pocket placement

¾ in (2 cm)

⅝ in (1.5 cm) crosshatch quilting

2 ⅜ in (6 cm)

Bottom

4 in (10 cm)

15 in (38 cm)

¾ in (2 cm)

Pocket placement

10¾ in (27 cm)

Pocket Panel (make 2)

½ in (1.2 cm)

Pocket opening

⅛ in (3 mm) quilting

4¼ in (11 cm)

Bottom edge

Finishing line

About 11 in (28 cm)

Cutting Instructions

Trace and cut out the template on page 110. Cut out the following fabric pieces, adding ¼ in (7 mm) seam allowance.

Hexagon fabric
- 166 hexagons

Cut out the following fabric pieces, which do not have templates, according to the measurements below (these measurements include seam allowance).

Batting
- Pocket panels (cut 2): 8¼ x 15 in (21 x 38 cm)
- Bag batting: 14¾ x 19 in (37 x 48 cm)

Muslin
- Pocket panel backing (cut 2): 8¼ x 15 in (21 x 38 cm)
- Bag muslin base: 14¾ x 19 in (37 x 48 cm)

Binding fabric
- Binding: 1½ yds (1.4 m) of 1¼ in (3 cm) wide single-fold bias binding

Bag fabric
- Bag top: 11¼ x 15½ in (28.4 x 39.4 cm)

Fusible interfacing
- Bag interfacing: 11¼ x 15½ in (28.4 x 39.4 cm)

Lining fabric
- Lining: 11¼ x 15½ in (28.4 x 39.4 cm)

Construction Steps

1. Make 166 hexies as shown in the guide on page 55. To make each pocket panel, sew 83 hexies together, following the layout shown in the diagram on page 108.

2. Layer each pocket panel, batting, and muslin backing. Mark the finishing lines and quilt as shown in the diagram on page 108. Trim the battings to match the size and shape of the pocket panels. Trim the muslin backings to match the shape of the pocket panels, leaving ¼ in (7 mm) seam allowance.

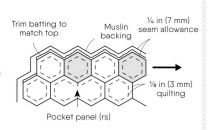

Trim batting to match top
Muslin backing
¼ in (7 mm) seam allowance
⅛ in (3 mm) quilting
Pocket panel (rs)

3. For each pocket panel, make clips into the muslin backing at the concave hexagon corners as shown in the diagram below. Stop clipping about 1 mm from the finishing line. Fold the backing seam allowance in so it aligns with the top. Slipstitch the top and backing together along the upper edge of the pocket panel (refer to page 62).

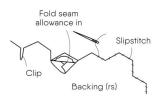

Fold seam allowance in
Slipstitch
Clip
Backing (rs)

Note: There's no need to finish the side or bottom edges of the pocket panel. The bottom will be bound in the next step and the sides will be finished when the bag is sewn together in step 8.

4. Bind the bottom edge of each pocket panel: With right sides together, align the binding with the finishing line along the bottom edge of each pocket panel. Sew along the marked finishing line. Trim the excess pocket panel fabric, leaving ¼ in (7 mm) seam allowance. Wrap the binding around the seam allowances and hand stitch to the muslin backing.

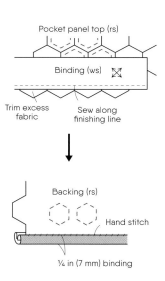

Pocket panel top (rs)
Binding (ws)
Trim excess fabric
Sew along finishing line
Backing (rs)
Hand stitch
¼ in (7 mm) binding

5. Layer the bag top, batting, and muslin base. Quilt as shown in the diagram on page 108. Trim the batting and muslin to match the size of the top. Adhere fusible interfacing to the muslin base.

Note: This bag is constructed with batting, a muslin base, and a layer of fusible interfacing to provide support and structure. A separate lining will be added to hide these layers. You could also use a foam interfacing instead and skip these steps.

6. With right sides together, align each pocket panel with the bag, following the placement noted in the diagram on page 108. **Note:** The pocket should be positioned with the bound edge at the top. Sew each pocket panel to the bag, stitching just below the binding.

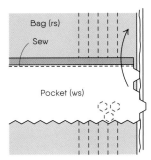

7. Fold the pocket panels up. Press in place so the binding is no longer visible. Topstitch each pocket panel to divide into thirds evenly. Each section should measure about 3½ in (9 cm) wide.

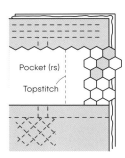

8. Fold the bag in half with right sides together. Sew together along the sides. Trim the excess pocket panel fabric along the sides, leaving ¼ in (7 mm) seam allowance.

9. Miter the corners: Press the side seams open. Align each side seam with the bottom fold. Sew across the corners with a 4 in (10 cm) seam. Trim the excess fabric, leaving ¼ in (7 mm) seam allowance.

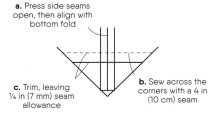

10. Make the lining: Fold the lining in half with right sides together. Sew together along the sides. Repeat step 9 to miter the corners. Insert the lining into the bag with wrong sides together. Baste together around the bag opening.

11. Align the wrong side of the handles with the lining so the handles are facing down (refer to the diagram on page 108 for handle placement). Sew the handles in place, taking care to stitch in the bag opening seam allowance. This will ensure that the raw edges of the handles are covered once the binding is attached.

12. Bind the opening (refer to page 92): With right sides together, sew the short ends of the binding to form a loop matching the size of the opening. With right sides together, sew the binding loop to the bag. Wrap the binding around the seam allowances and hand stitch to the lining.

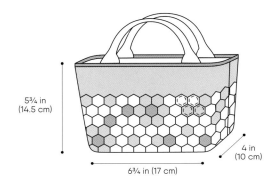

Full-Size Template

Note: This template should be used for piecing the hexies. Add ¼ in (7 mm) seam allowance to cut out each hexie.

ROSETTE BASKET BAG

Shown on page 23

Materials

FOR THE BAG

- **Hexagon fabric:** 12 assorted print scraps
- **Accent fabric:** 1 yd (1 m) of solid brown
- **Lining fabric:** ½ yd (0.5 m)
- ½ yd (0.5 m) of muslin
- **Batting:** 15¾ x 43¼ in (40 x 110 cm)
- **Fusible interfacing:** 15¾ x 43¼ in (40 x 110 cm)
- 1 yd (1 m) of ¼ in (5 mm) diameter leather cord
- One set of 16 in (40 cm) handles
- ¾ yd (0.7 m) of floral trim
- 1 yd (1 m) of 2 in (5 cm) wide faux fur trim
- 5¼ x 10¼ in (13 x 26 cm) of plastic sheeting
- (123) ⅝ in (1.6 cm) hexagon precut EPP shapes

FOR THE OPTIONAL CORSAGE

- **Rose fabric:** 12 in (30.5 cm) squares of solid pink and pink print
- **Leaf fabric:** 12 in (30.5 cm) square of green print
- ¾ yd (0.7 m) of 1¼ in (3 cm) wide ribbon
- Three 12 in (30.5 cm) long pieces of rickrack
- One safety pin
- Clover Sweetheart Rose Maker

> Sew using ¼ in (7 mm) seam allowance, unless otherwise noted.

Project Diagram

Diagrams show finished measurements (seam allowance not included).

Bag

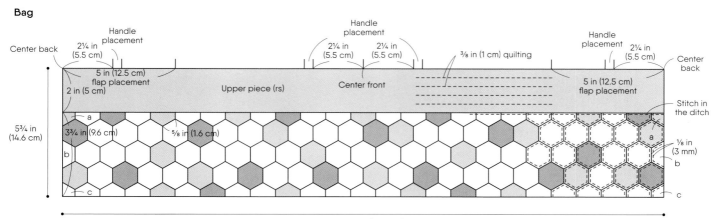

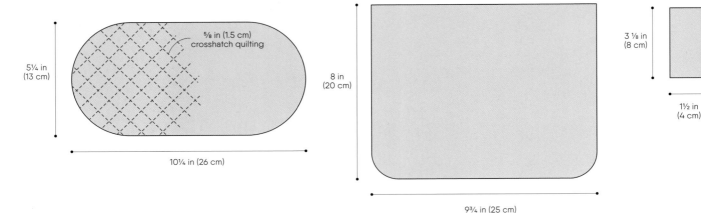

Bottom

⅝ in (1.5 cm) crosshatch quilting

5¼ in (13 cm)

10¼ in (26 cm)

Flap

8 in (20 cm)

9¾ in (25 cm)

Handle Loops

3 ⅛ in (8 cm)

1½ in (4 cm)

Cutting Instructions for the Bag

Trace and cut out the templates on Pattern Sheet A. Cut out the following fabric pieces, adding ¼ in (7 mm) seam allowance.

Hexagon fabric
- 123 hexagons

Lining fabric
- 1 flap lining

Accent fabric
- 1 flap

Lining fabric
- 1 bottom

Fusible interfacing
- 1 bottom

Cut out the following fabric piece, adding ¾ in (2 cm) seam allowance.

Muslin
- 1 bottom plate fabric

Cut out the following piece without adding seam allowance.

Plastic sheeting
- 1 bottom plate

Cut the following pieces a few inches larger than the template on each side. They will be trimmed into shape once the layers have been quilted.

Accent fabric
- 1 bottom

Batting
- 1 bottom

Muslin
- 1 bottom muslin base

Cut out the following fabric pieces, which do not have templates, according to the measurements below (these measurements include seam allowance).

Accent fabric
- Upper piece: 2½ x 27 in (6.4 x 68.2 cm)
- Inside facing: 2½ x 27 in (6.4 x 68.2 cm)
- Binding: 1 yd (1 m) of 1¼ in (3 cm) wide single-fold bias binding
- Handle loops (cut 4): 1½ x 3 ⅛ in (4 x 8 cm)

Batting
- Bag batting: 9¾ x 30½ in (24.6 x 76.8 cm)

Muslin
- Bag muslin base: 9¾ x 30½ in (24.6 x 76.8 cm)

Fusible interfacing
- Bag interfacing: 6¼ x 27 in (16 x 68.2 cm)

Lining fabric
- Bag lining: 4¼ x 27 in (11 x 68.2 cm)

Cutting Instructions for the Optional Corsage

For the Roses
Use the Clover Sweetheart Rose Maker template to cut two rectangles from each fabric, adding ⅜ in (1 cm) seam allowance.

For the Leaves
From the leaf fabric, cut two small circles and four large circles (see Pattern Sheet A for templates).

Construction Steps

1. Make 123 hexies as shown in the guide on page 55. Sew the hexies together as shown in the diagram on page 111. Make sure to use the same fabrics for the hexies marked a, b, and c as they will align when the bag is sewn together.

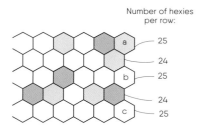

Number of hexies per row:
- 25
- 24
- 25
- 24
- 25

2. With right sides together, sew the upper piece to the hexie panel to complete the bag top.

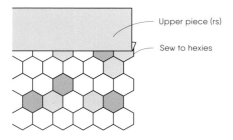

Upper piece (rs)

Sew to hexies

3. Layer the bag top, batting and muslin base. Mark the finishing lines and quilt as shown in the diagram on page 111. Trim into shape, leaving ¼ in (7 mm) seam allowance. Adhere fusible interfacing to the muslin base.

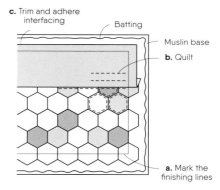

c. Trim and adhere interfacing

Batting

Muslin base

b. Quilt

a. Mark the finishing lines

Note: This bag is constructed with batting, a muslin base and a layer of fusible interfacing to provide support and structure. A separate lining will be added to hide these layers. You could also use a foam interfacing instead and skip these steps.

4. Layer the bottom, batting and muslin base. Quilt as shown in the diagram on page 112. Trim into shape, leaving ¼ in (7 mm) seam allowance. Adhere fusible interfacing to the muslin base.

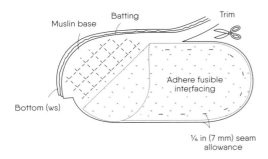

Muslin base
Batting
Trim
Adhere fusible interfacing
Bottom (ws)
¼ in (7 mm) seam allowance

5. Fold the bag in half with right sides together and sew. With right sides together, sew the bottom to the bag, leaving a ⅜ in (1 cm) opening at the seam for the cord ends.

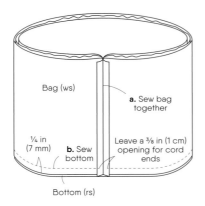

Bag (ws)
a. Sew bag together
¼ in (7 mm)
b. Sew bottom
Leave a ⅜ in (1 cm) opening for cord ends
Bottom (rs)

6. Turn the bag right side out. Hand stitch the cord to the bottom seam. Insert the cord ends into the opening

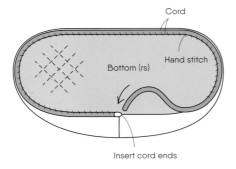

Cord
Hand stitch
Bottom (rs)
Insert cord ends

7. Sew the opening closed, stitching through the cords. Trim the excess cord.

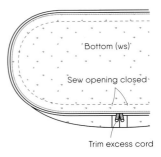

Bottom (ws)
Sew opening closed
Trim excess cord

8. Make the bottom plate as shown below, then hand stitch it in place on the inside of the bag.

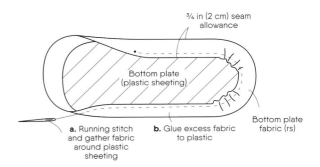

¾ in (2 cm) seam allowance
Bottom plate (plastic sheeting)
Bottom plate fabric (rs)
a. Running stitch and gather fabric around plastic sheeting
b. Glue excess fabric to plastic

9. Fold and press the long edges of each handle loop piece ⅜ in (1 cm) to the wrong side. Fold and press each handle loop piece in half with right sides facing out. Press, then topstitch along the long edges. Thread each loop through a handle end, then sew to the bag inside, following the placement noted in the diagram on page 111.

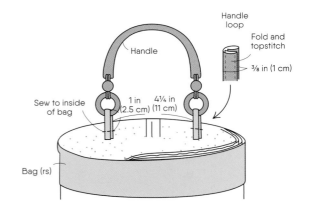

Handle loop
Handle
Fold and topstitch
⅜ in (1 cm)
Sew to inside of bag
1 in (2.5 cm)
4¼ in (11 cm)
Bag (rs)

10. Make the flap: Sew the flap and flap lining with right sides together, leaving the top open. Turn right side out.

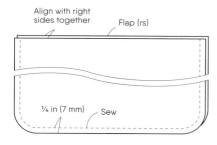

Align with right sides together

Flap (rs)

¼ in (7 mm)

Sew

11. Attach the flap to the bag: Sew the floral trim to the right side of the flap. Align the right side of the flap with the inside of the bag, following the placement noted below (also refer to the diagram on page 111). Sew the flap in place.

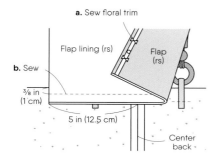

a. Sew floral trim

Flap lining (rs)

Flap (rs)

b. Sew

³⁄₈ in (1 cm)

5 in (12.5 cm)

Center back

12. Make the lining: With right sides together, sew the inside facing to the bag lining. Fold the bag lining in half with right sides together and sew. Sew the bottom lining to the bag lining.

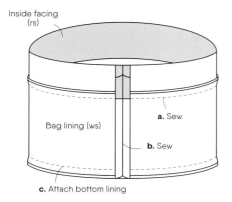

Inside facing (rs)

Bag lining (ws)

a. Sew

b. Sew

c. Attach bottom lining

13. Insert the lining into the bag with wrong sides together. Baste together around the bag opening. Take care to pull the flap away from the bag so it doesn't get trapped underneath the lining.

14. Bind the opening (refer to page 92): With right sides together, sew the short ends of the binding to form a loop matching the size of the opening. With right sides together, sew the binding loop to the bag. Wrap the binding around the seam allowances and hand stitch to the lining.

15. Sew the short ends of the faux fur trim together to form a loop matching the size of the bag opening. Position the loop on the outside of the bag, so it covers the upper piece. Hand stitch the faux fur in place.

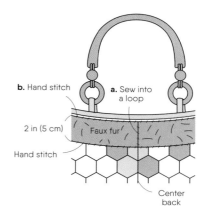

b. Hand stitch

a. Sew into a loop

2 in (5 cm)

Faux fur

Hand stitch

Center back

16. If desired, make the corsage as shown on page 116.

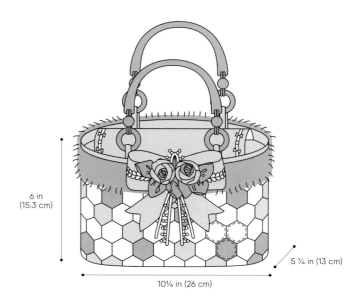

6 in (15.3 cm)

5 ¼ in (13 cm)

10¼ in (26 cm)

HOW TO MAKE THE CORSAGE

Note: This corsage is made using the Clover Sweetheart Rose Maker. Follow the manufacturer's instructions to make the roses.

Make the Roses

1. Layer one of the pieces of solid fabric between the top and base templates with the wrong side facing up.

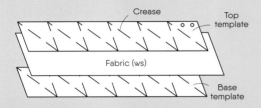

2. Insert a pin through the holes in the templates. Fold along the template's first crease. Running stitch the two layers of fabric together along the edge of the template.

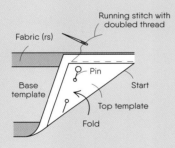

3. Fold the fabric into shape along the creases. Running stitch as you work.

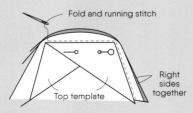

4. Remove the two templates (one will be inside the fabric tube). Trim the seam allowances to ¼ in (5 mm). Turn the tube right side out.

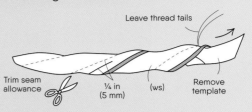

5. Pull the thread tails to gather the tube. Fold the ends in and hand stitch closed. Insert the tip of the fabric tube into a bobby pin. Repeat steps 1–5 with one of the print fabrics.

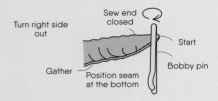

6. Roll the solid fabric into a tight rose around the bobby pin. Using the thread tails, stitch through the base to hold the flower together.

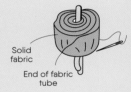

7. Overlap the print fabric tube with the end of the solid fabric and wrap around the rose. Use a tweezer to adjust the shape of the flower and extract the bobby pin. Stitch through the base to hold the flower together.

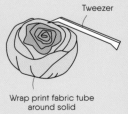

Repeat steps 1–7 to make another rose.

Make the Leaves

1. Starting with the wrong side facing up, fold each circle in half.

2. Fold in half again.

3. Running stitch along the curved edge using ⅛ in (3 mm) seam allowance. Stitch through all layers of the fabric.

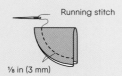

4. Pull the thread tails and squeeze the fabric to gather into a leaf shape.

5. Sew three leaves to the wrong side of each rose.

Assemble the Corsage

1. Sew one piece of rickrack to the center of the ribbon. Overlap the ends of the ribbon as shown to form a bow shape. Running stitch the bow together at the center. Pull the thread tails to gather the bow into shape.

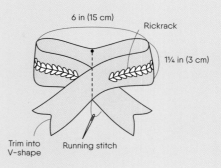

2. Align the remaining two pieces of rickrack. Fold in half. Tie a knot to hold the fold in place.

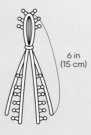

3. Sew the folded rickrack to the center of the bow. Next, sew the roses on top. Sew a safety pin to the back of the bow.

DIAMONDS & LACE POUCH

Shown on page 25

Materials

- **Diamond fabric:** 10 assorted print scraps
- **Accent fabric:** One fat quarter of solid linen
- **Lining fabric:** One fat eighth
- One fat quarter of muslin
- **Batting:** 14¼ x 16½ in (36 x 41.5 cm)
- One 12 in (30.5 cm) zipper
- ¾ yd (0.7 m) of ⅛ in (3 mm) diameter cord

- ⅜ yd (0.4 m) of 2 ⅜ in (6 cm) wide lace
- ¾ yd (0.7 m) of rickrack
- 92 small beads
- (134) 1 in (2.6 cm) diamond precut EPP shapes
- **Bow fabric (optional):** 6¼ x 37 in (16 x 94 cm) of dark pink print

Sew using ¼ in (7 mm) seam allowance, unless otherwise noted.

Project Diagram

Diagrams show finished measurements (seam allowance not included).

Clutch

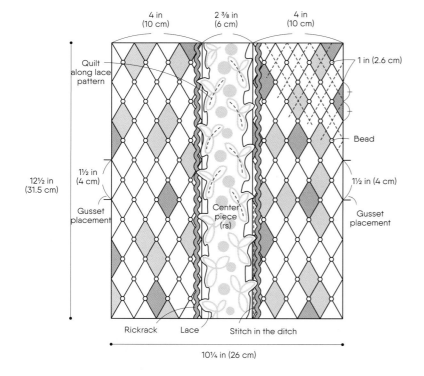

4 in (10 cm) 2 ⅜ in (6 cm) 4 in (10 cm)

Quilt along lace pattern

1 in (2.6 cm)

Bead

12½ in (31.5 cm)

1½ in (4 cm)

Gusset placement

Center piece (rs)

1½ in (4 cm)

Gusset placement

Rickrack   Lace   Stitch in the ditch

10¼ in (26 cm)

Gusset (make 2)

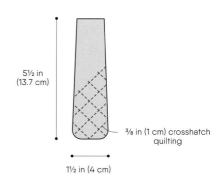

5½ in (13.7 cm)

⅜ in (1 cm) crosshatch quilting

1½ in (4 cm)

Cutting Instructions

Trace and cut out the templates on page 120 and Pattern Sheet A. Cut out the following fabric pieces, adding ¼ in (7 mm) seam allowance.

Diamond fabric
- 134 diamonds

Accent fabric
- 2 gussets

Batting
- 2 gussets*

Muslin
- 2 gusset muslin bases*

Lining fabric
- 2 gussets

*Cut the gusset battings and muslin bases out a few inches larger than the template on each side. They will be trimmed into shape once the layers have been quilted.

Cut out the following fabric pieces, which do not have templates, according to the measurements below (these measurements include seam allowance).

Accent fabric
- Center piece: 2 ⅞ x 13 in (7.4 x 32.9 cm)
- Binding: 1 yd (1 m) of 1¼ in (3 cm) wide single-fold bias binding

Batting
- Clutch batting: 14¼ x 16½ in (36 x 41.5 cm)

Muslin
- Clutch muslin base: 14¼ x 16½ in (36 x 41.5 cm)

Lining fabric
- Clutch lining: 10¾ x 13 in (27.4 x 32.9 cm)

Construction Steps

1. Make 134 diamonds as shown in the guide on page 63. To make each panel, sew 67 diamonds together as shown below (also refer to page 65).

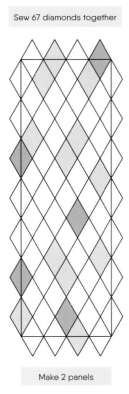

Sew 67 diamonds together

Make 2 panels

2. With right sides together, sew a panel to each side of the center piece. This will be the clutch top.

3. Layer the top, batting, and muslin base. Quilt as shown in the diagram on page 118. Appliqué the lace to the center piece. Sew the rickrack along each edge of the center piece. Sew a bead to each diamond point. Mark the finishing lines, then trim into shape, leaving ¼ in (7 mm) seam allowance.

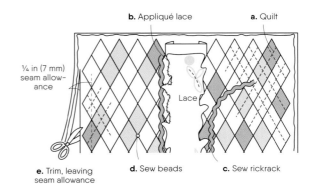

b. Appliqué lace   a. Quilt

¼ in (7 mm) seam allowance

Lace

e. Trim, leaving seam allowance   d. Sew beads   c. Sew rickrack

4. Make the gussets: Layer each gusset, batting, and muslin base. Quilt as shown in the diagram on page 118. Use the template to trim the gussets into shape, leaving ¼ in (7 mm) seam allowance.

5. Fold the clutch in half with right sides together and sew the gussets to the clutch.

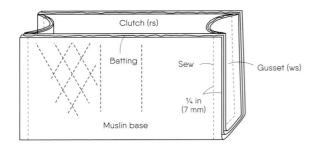

6. Turn the clutch right side out. Hand stitch the cord to the gusset seams.

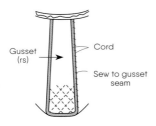

7. Make the lining: Fold the clutch lining in half with right sides together and sew the gusset linings to the clutch lining. Insert the lining into the clutch with wrong sides together. Baste together around the clutch opening.

8. Bind the opening (refer to page 79): With right sides together, sew the short ends of the binding to form a loop matching the size of the opening. With right sides together, sew the binding loop to the clutch. Wrap the binding around the seam allowances and hand stitch to the lining.

9. Hand stitch the zipper to the binding on the inside of the clutch. The stitches should not be visible on the outside of the clutch. Note that the zipper end should extend beyond the opening, as shown in the finished diagram below.

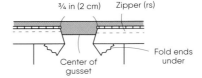

10. If desired, make the bow as shown on page 127. Hand stitch the bow to the clutch.

Finished Diagram

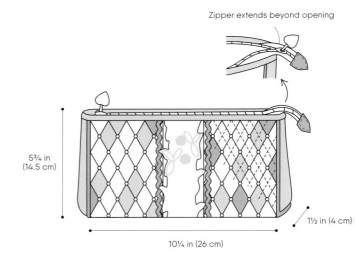

Full-Size Template

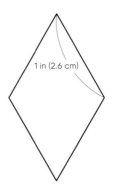

Note: This template should be used for piecing the diamonds. Add ¼ in (7 mm) seam allowance to cut out each diamond.

TWINKLING STARS TABLE MAT

Shown on page 26

Materials

- **Hexagon fabric:** Scraps of lace or other fabric
- **Diamond fabric:** Six assorted print scraps in each green, beige, and pink
- **Background fabric:** ⅝ yd (0.6 m) of floral print
- **Backing fabric:** ⅝ yd (0.6 m)
- **Batting:** 23 in (58 cm) square

- Scraps of lightweight fusible interfacing (only if using lace fabric for hexies)
- 2½ yds (2.3 m) of 1 in (2.5 cm) wide lace
- (24) 1 in (2.6 cm) hexagon precut EPP shapes
- (78) 1 in (2.6 cm) diamond precut EPP shapes

Sew using ¼ in (7 mm) seam allowance, unless otherwise noted.

Project Diagram

Diagrams show finished measurements (seam allowance not included).

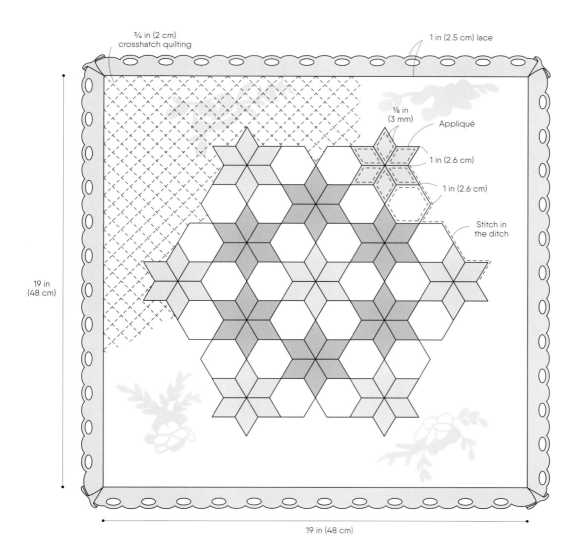

¾ in (2 cm) crosshatch quilting

1 in (2.5 cm) lace

⅛ in (3 mm)

Appliqué

1 in (2.6 cm)

1 in (2.6 cm)

Stitch in the ditch

19 in (48 cm)

19 in (48 cm)

Cutting Instructions

Trace and cut out the templates on Pattern Sheet B. Cut out the following fabric pieces, adding ¼ in (7 mm) seam allowance.

Hexagon fabric

- 24 hexagons

Lightweight fusible interfacing

- 24 hexagons (only if using lace fabric for hexies)

Diamond fabric

- 78 diamonds

Cut out the following fabric pieces, which do not have templates, according to the measurements below (these measurements include seam allowance).

Background fabric

- Mat background: 23 in (58 cm) square

Batting

- Mat batting: 23 in (58 cm) square

Backing fabric

- Mat backing: 23 in (58 cm) square

Construction Steps

1. If using lace for the hexies, adhere lightweight fusible interfacing to the wrong side of each hexie. Make 24 hexies as shown in the guide on page 55.

2. Make 78 diamonds as shown in the guide on page 63.

3. To make each star motif, sew six diamonds together as shown below (also refer to page 65). Make 13 star motifs total.

Sew 6 diamonds together

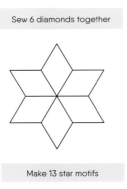

Make 13 star motifs

4. Sew the star motifs and hexagons together, following the layout shown in diagram on page 121.

5. Appliqué the assembled EPP motif to the mat background.

6. On the wrong side of the mat, trim the background fabric from behind the appliqué, leaving ¼ in (7 mm) seam allowance.

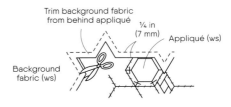

Trim background fabric from behind appliqué

¼ in (7 mm)

Appliqué (ws)

Background fabric (ws)

7. Layer the mat top, batting, and backing. Mark the quilting and finishing lines. Quilt as shown in the diagram on page 121. Take care not to quilt the areas 1¼ in (3 cm) from the finishing lines. Trim the excess fabric, leaving ¼ in (7 mm) seam allowance. Trim the batting only along the finishing line.

8. Insert the lace between the top and the backing layers. Baste in place. Whipstitch the short ends of the lace together (see page 57). Fold and press the seam allowances under on both the top and backing. Hand stitch the backing to the lace. Finish quilting the areas left unfinished in step 7.

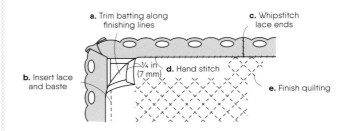

a. Trim batting along finishing lines

c. Whipstitch lace ends

b. Insert lace and baste

¼ in (7 mm)

d. Hand stitch

e. Finish quilting

STAR MINI QUILT

Shown on page 27

Materials

- **Diamond/appliqué fabric:** 34 assorted print scraps in green, beige, and pink
- **Border fabric #1:** One fat quarter of pink solid
- **Border fabric #2:** ¾ yd (0.7 m) of green print
- **Backing fabric:** 1 yd (1 m)

- **Batting:** 27¼ in (69 cm) square
- (78) ⅞ in (2.2 cm) diamond precut EPP shapes
- White yarn for trapunto quilting

Sew using ¼ in (7 mm) seam allowance, unless otherwise noted.

Project Diagram

Diagrams show finished measurements (seam allowance not included).

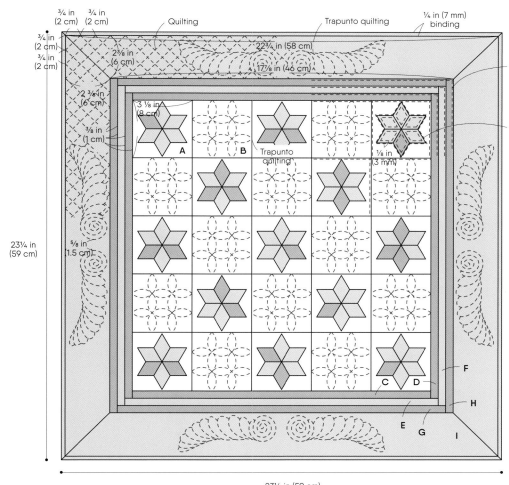

Full-Size Template

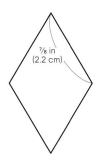

Note: This template should be used for piecing the diamonds. Add ¼ in (7 mm) seam allowance to cut out each diamond.

Cutting Instructions

Trace and cut out the template on page 123. Cut out the following fabric pieces, adding ¼ in (7 mm) seam allowance.

Diamond/appliqué fabric

- 78 diamonds

Cut out the following fabric pieces, which do not have templates, according to the measurements below (these measurements include seam allowance).

Diamond/appliqué fabric

- A (cut 13): 3⅝ in (9.4 cm) squares
- B (cut 12): 3⅝ in (9.4 cm) squares

Border fabric #1

- C borders (cut 2): ⅞ x 16⅛ in (2.4 x 41.4 cm)
- D borders (cut 2): ⅞ x 16⅞ in (2.4 x 43.4 cm)
- G borders (cut 2): ⅞ x 17⅝ in (2.4 x 45.4 cm)
- H borders (cut 2): ⅞ x 18⅜ in (2.4 x 47.4 cm)

Border fabric #2

- E borders (cut 2): ⅞ x 16⅞ in (2.4 x 43.4 cm)
- F borders (cut 2): ⅞ x 17⅝ in (2.4 x 45.4 cm)
- I borders (cut 4): 2⅞ x 29 in (7.4 x 73.5 cm)
- Binding: 2¾ yds (2.5 m) of 1¼ in (3 cm) wide single-fold bias binding

Batting

- Quilt batting: 27¼ in (69 cm) square

Backing fabric

- Quilt backing: 27¼ in (69 cm) square

Construction Steps

1. Make 78 diamonds as shown in the guide on page 63. To make each star motif, sew six diamonds together as shown below (also refer to page 65). Make 13 star motifs total. Appliqué each star motif to an A square.

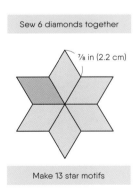

Sew 6 diamonds together

⅞ in (2.2 cm)

Make 13 star motifs

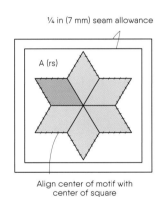

¼ in (7 mm) seam allowance

A (rs)

Align center of motif with center of square

2. With right sides together, alternately sew A and B squares into five rows of five. Sew the five rows together as shown in the diagram on page 123.

3. Sew borders C–H to the quilt top using the same process as making a log cabin block (refer to page 53). Refer to page 51 for instructions on attaching the mitered I borders.

4. Layer the quilt top, batting, and backing. Quilt as shown in the diagram on page 123.

5. Bind the quilt (refer to page 45).

6. Finish the I borders with trapunto quilting (refer to the diagram on page 123 for placement). **Note:** There are quilting templates on Pattern Sheet B.

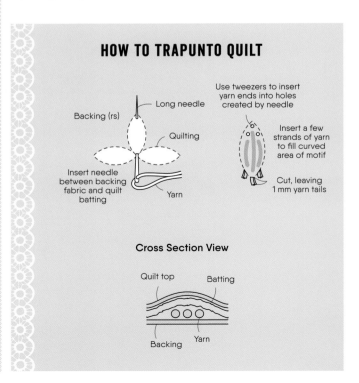

HOW TO TRAPUNTO QUILT

Backing (rs)

Long needle

Quilting

Insert needle between backing fabric and quilt batting

Yarn

Use tweezers to insert yarn ends into holes created by needle

Insert a few strands of yarn to fill curved area of motif

Cut, leaving 1 mm yarn tails

Cross Section View

Quilt top

Batting

Backing

Yarn

BOW TIE CLUTCH

Shown on page 29

Materials

- **Apple core fabric:** Seven assorted fat eighths
- **Bow fabric:** ¼ yd (0.25 m) of metallic linen
- **Lining fabric:** One fat quarter of floral print linen
- ½ yd (0.5 m) of muslin

- **Batting:** 15 x 23 in (38 x 58 cm)
- 1¾ yd (1.6 m) of ⅛ in (3 mm) diameter cord
- One magnetic button set
- (135) 2 in (5 cm) apple core precut EPP shapes

Project Diagram

Diagrams show finished measurements (seam allowance not included).

Sew using ¼ in (7 mm) seam allowance, unless otherwise noted.

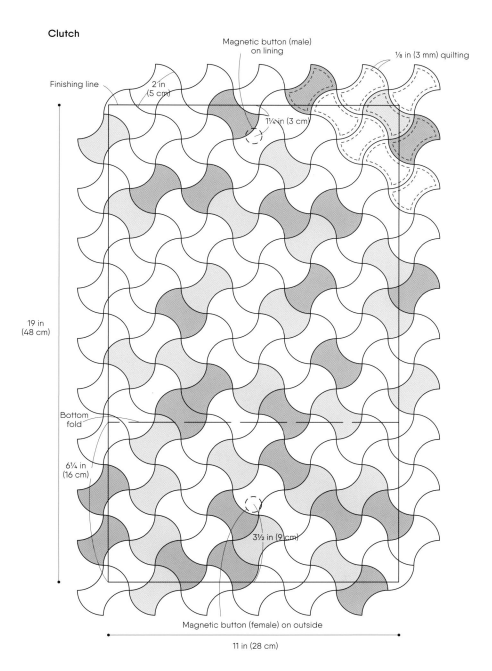

Clutch

Magnetic button (male) on lining

⅛ in (3 mm) quilting

Finishing line

2 in (5 cm)

1¼ in (3 cm)

19 in (48 cm)

Bottom fold

6¼ in (16 cm)

3½ in (9 cm)

Magnetic button (female) on outside

11 in (28 cm)

Cutting Instructions

Trace and cut out the template on page 127. Cut out the following fabric pieces, adding ¼ in (7 mm) seam allowance.

Apple core fabric

- 135 apple cores

Cut out the following fabric pieces, which do not have templates, according to the measurements below (these measurements include seam allowance).

Batting

- Clutch batting: 15 x 23 in (38 x 58 cm)

Muslin

- Muslin base: 15 x 23 in (38 x 58 cm)

Lining fabric

- Clutch lining: 11½ x 19½ in (29.4 x 49.4 cm)

Bow fabric

- Bow: 6¼ x 33¼ in (16 x 84 cm)
- Bow center: 3½ x 4 in (9 x 10 cm)

Construction Steps

1. Make 135 apple cores as shown in the guide on page 66.

2. Sew the apple cores together to create the clutch top, following the layout shown in the diagram on page 125.

3. Layer the clutch top, batting, and muslin base. Mark the finishing lines. Quilt as shown in the diagram on page 125. Trim into shape, leaving ¼ in (7 mm) seam allowance.

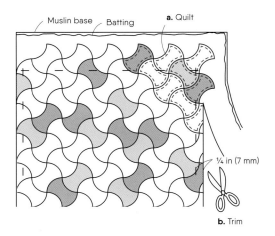

Muslin base   Batting   **a.** Quilt

¼ in (7 mm)

b. Trim

4. Align the clutch and lining with right sides together. Sew around all four sides, leaving a 4 in (10 cm) opening along the top and a ⅜ in (1 cm) opening along one side for the cord ends (see diagram below for placement). Turn right side out.

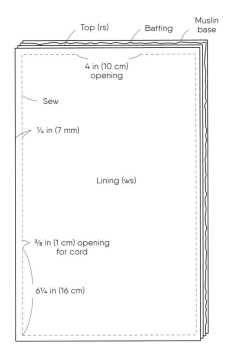

Top (rs)   Batting   Muslin base

4 in (10 cm) opening

Sew

¼ in (7 mm)

Lining (ws)

⅜ in (1 cm) opening for cord

6¼ in (16 cm)

5. Hand stitch the 4 in (10 cm) opening closed. Hand stitch the cord to the seams. Insert the cord ends into the opening, then sew it closed.

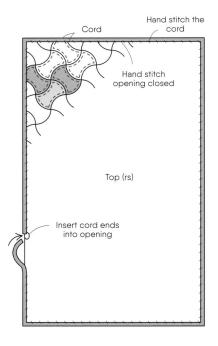

Cord   Hand stitch the cord

Hand stitch opening closed

Top (rs)

Insert cord ends into opening

6. Fold the bottom third of the clutch up. Hand stitch the fold in place along the left and right edges of the clutch, making your stitches through the cords on the inside of the bag. Sew the magnetic button components to the clutch following the placement noted in the diagram below.

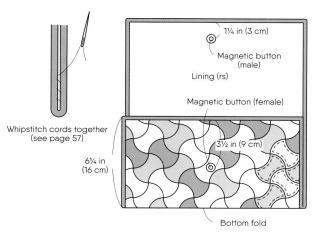

7. Make the bow and sew it to the front of the clutch.

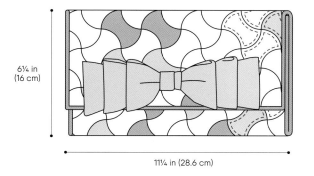

Full-Size Template

Note: This template should be used for piecing the apple cores. Add ¼ in (7 mm) seam allowance to cut out each apple core.

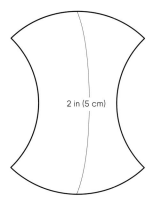

HOW TO MAKE THE BOW

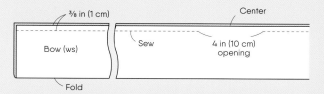

1. Fold the bow in half with right sides together. Sew along one long edge, leaving a 4 in (10 cm) opening at the center.

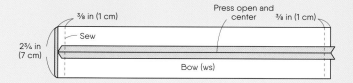

2. Press the seam allowance open and center it along the back. Sew the short edges closed.

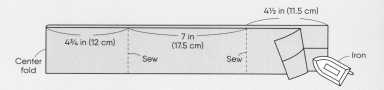

3. Turn right side out. Fold the ribbon in half and press into shape. Topstitch through both layers to divide into three sections.

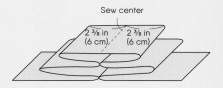

4. Starting from the center fold, separate the two layers for each section. This will create three tiers. Topstitch along the center to hold all the layers together.

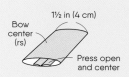

5. Fold the bow center in half with right sides together, aligning the shorter edges. Sew, then press the seam allowance open. Turn right side out. Center the seam allowance along the back.

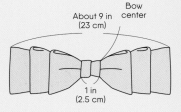

6. Wrap the bow center around the topstitched seam from step 4. Hand stitch the short edges of the bow center together to hold it in place.

APPLE CORE TOTE

Shown on page 30

Materials

- **Patchwork fabric:** Nine print fat quarters
- **Bottom/binding fabric:** ⅝ yd (0.6 m) of linen
- **Lining fabric:** ¾ yd (0.7 m)
- ¾ yd (0.7 m) of muslin
- **Batting:** 23¾ x 43¼ in (60 x 110 cm)
- **Fusible interfacing:** 19¾ x 39½ in (50 x 100 cm)
- 39½ in (100 cm) of ⅛ in (3 mm) diameter cord

- 6 x 10¼ in (15 x 26 cm) of plastic sheeting (for bottom plate)
- One set of 16½ in (42 cm) handles
- One ⅝ in (1.5 cm) diameter magnetic button
- One ⅞ in (2.2 cm) diameter cover button
- (108) 2¾ in (7 cm) apple core precut EPP shapes

Sew using ¼ in (7 mm) seam allowance, unless otherwise noted.

Project Diagram

Diagrams show finished measurements (seam allowance not included).

Bag Outsides (make 2)

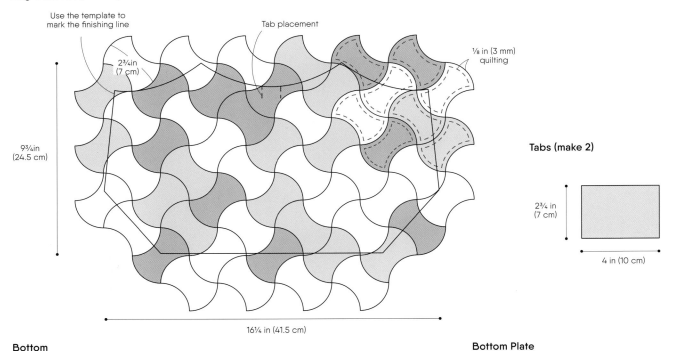

Use the template to mark the finishing line

Tab placement

2¾ in (7 cm)

⅛ in (3 mm) quilting

9¾ in (24.5 cm)

16¼ in (41.5 cm)

Tabs (make 2)

2¾ in (7 cm)

4 in (10 cm)

Bottom

6¼ in (16 cm)

⅝ in (1.5 cm) quilting

Opening for cord ends

16¼ in (41 cm)

Bottom Plate

Plastic sheeting

6 in (15 cm)

10¼ in (26 cm)

Cutting Instructions

Trace and cut out the templates on Pattern Sheet B. Cut out the following fabric pieces, adding ¼ in (7 mm) seam allowance.

Patchwork fabric

- 108 apple cores

Batting

- 2 bag outsides*
- 1 bottom*

Muslin

- 2 bag outside muslin bases*
- 1 bottom muslin base*

Fusible interfacing

- 2 bag outsides
- 1 bottom

Bottom/binding fabric

- 1 bottom*
- 1 covered button

Lining fabric

- 2 bag outsides
- 1 bottom

*Cut these pieces out a few inches larger than the template on each side. The bottom will be trimmed into shape once the layers have been quilted.

Cut out the following fabric pieces, which do not have templates, according to the measurements below (these measurements include seam allowance).

Plastic sheeting

- Bottom plate: 6 x 10¼ in (15 x 26 cm)

Muslin

- Bottom plate fabric: 7½ x 11¾ in (19 x 30 cm)

Lining fabric

- Inside pocket: 6⅝ x 7 in (16.5 x 18 cm)

Bottom/binding fabric

- Tabs (cut 2): 2¾ x 4 in (7 x 10 cm)
- Binding: 1½ yds (1.4 m) of 1½ in (4 cm) wide single-fold bias binding

Construction Steps

1. Make 108 apple cores as shown in the guide on page 66. Sew them together to make two bag outsides. Use the template on Pattern Sheet B to mark the finishing lines.

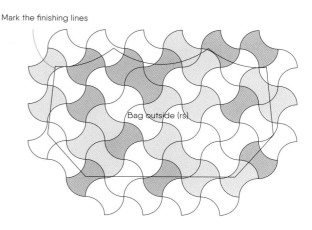

Mark the finishing lines

Bag outside (rs)

2. Make the bag outsides: Layer each bag outside, batting, and muslin base. Quilt as shown below. Trim into shape, leaving ¼ in (7 mm) seam allowance. Adhere fusible interfacing to each muslin base.

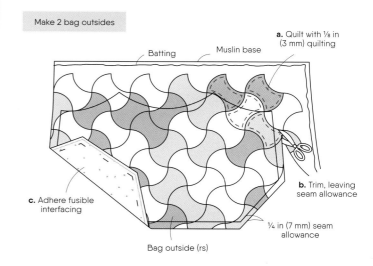

Make 2 bag outsides

Batting

Muslin base

a. Quilt with ⅛ in (3 mm) quilting

b. Trim, leaving seam allowance

¼ in (7 mm) seam allowance

c. Adhere fusible interfacing

Bag outside (rs)

Note: This bag is constructed with batting, a muslin base, and layer of fusible interfacing to provide support and structure. A separate lining will be added to hide these layers. You could also use a foam interfacing instead and skip these steps.

3. Align the bag outsides with right sides together. Sew together along each side.

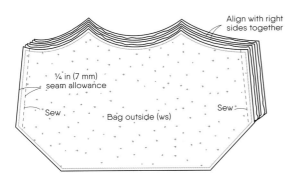

4. Make the bottom: Layer the bottom, batting and muslin base. Quilt as shown in the diagram on page 128. Use the template to trim the bottom into shape, leaving ¼ in (7 mm) seam allowance. Adhere fusible interfacing to the muslin base.

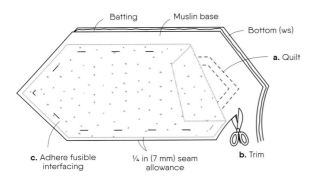

5. Align the bottom and bag outside with right sides together. Sew, leaving a ⅜ in (1 cm) opening for the cord ends.

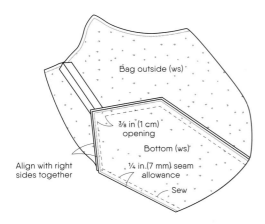

6. Turn the bag right side out. Sew the cord to the bottom seam. Insert the cord ends into the opening, then sew it closed. Make the bottom plate as shown below, then hand stitch it in place on the inside of the bag.

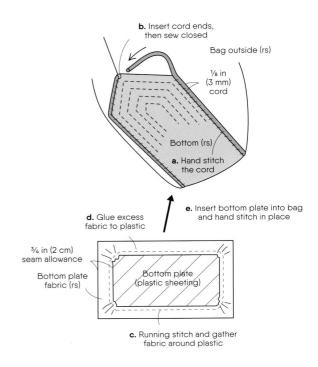

7. Make the inside pocket (refer to page 92): Fold and press the seam allowance under ⅜ in (1 cm) on each side. Fold and press the top edge under an additional ⅝ in (1.5 cm). Topstitch the pocket to one of the bag lining pieces, following the placement noted on the template.

8. Make the bag lining: Align the two lining pieces with right sides together. Sew together along each side. Sew the bottom lining to the bag lining.

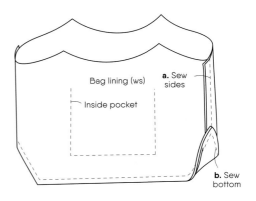

9. Insert the lining into the bag with wrong sides together. Baste around the bag opening. Make the tabs as shown and baste to the lining. Bind the bag opening as shown below.

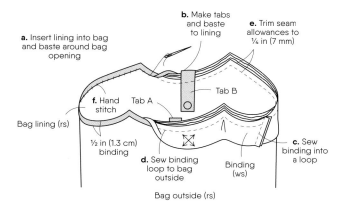

a. Insert lining into bag and baste around bag opening

b. Make tabs and baste to lining

e. Trim seam allowances to ¼ in (7 mm)

f. Hand stitch

Tab A

Tab B

Bag lining (rs)

½ in (1.3 cm) binding

d. Sew binding loop to bag outside

Binding (ws)

c. Sew binding into a loop

Bag outside (rs)

10. Sew the handles to the bag outside following placement noted in diagram below.

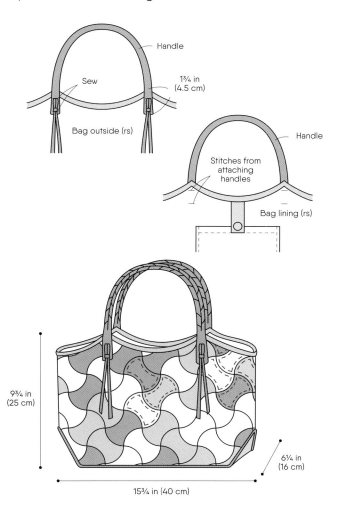

Handle

Sew

1¾ in (4.5 cm)

Bag outside (rs)

Handle

Stitches from attaching handles

Bag lining (rs)

9¾ in (25 cm)

6¼ in (16 cm)

15¾ in (40 cm)

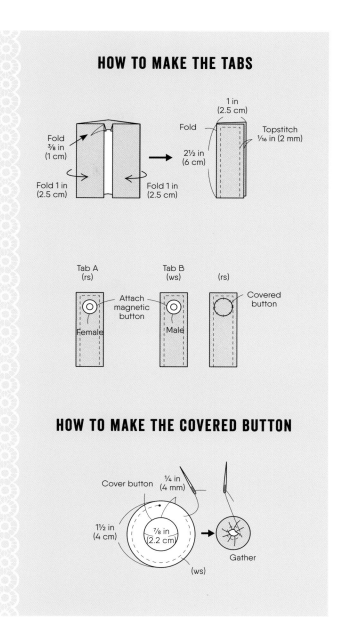

HOW TO MAKE THE TABS

Fold ⅜ in (1 cm)

Fold 1 in (2.5 cm)

Fold 1 in (2.5 cm)

1 in (2.5 cm)

Fold

2½ in (6 cm)

Topstitch ¹⁄₁₆ in (2 mm)

Tab A (rs)

Attach magnetic button

Female

Tab B (ws)

Male

(rs)

Covered button

HOW TO MAKE THE COVERED BUTTON

Cover button

¼ in (4 mm)

1½ in (4 cm)

⅞ in (2.2 cm)

(ws)

Gather

APPLE CORE MINI PURSE

Shown on page 31

Materials

- **Apple core fabric:** Nine assorted print scraps
- **Yoyo fabric:** Fat eighth of organdy
- **Lining fabric:** One fat quarter
- One fat quarter of muslin
- Six ¼ in (6 mm) diameter beads
- ¾ yd (0.7 m) of 1¼ in (3 cm) wide chenille trim
- One set of 1¼ x 15¾ in (3 x 40 cm) handles)
- (84) 2 in (5 cm) apple core precut EPP shapes

Sew using ¼ in (7 mm) seam allowance, unless otherwise noted.

Project Diagram

Diagrams show finished measurements (seam allowance not included).

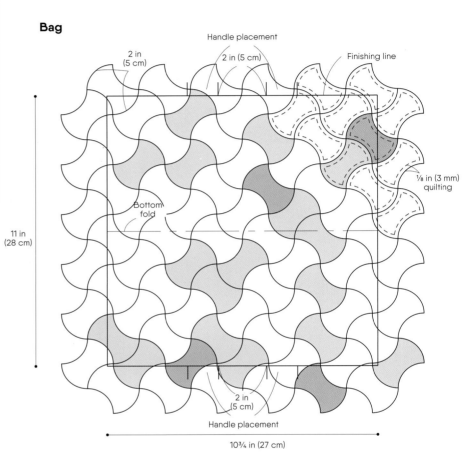

Bag

Handle placement

2 in (5 cm)

2 in (5 cm)

Finishing line

⅛ in (3 mm) quilting

Bottom fold

11 in (28 cm)

2 in (5 cm)

Handle placement

10¾ in (27 cm)

Cutting Instructions

Trace and cut out the templates on Pattern Sheet B.

Cut out the following fabric pieces, adding ¼ in (7 mm) seam allowance.

Apple core fabric

- 84 apple cores

Do not add seam allowance when cutting out the following pieces.

Yoyo fabric

- 12 yoyos

Cut out the following fabric pieces, which do not have templates, according to the measurements below (these measurements include seam allowance).

Batting

- Bag batting: 14¾ x 15 in (37 x 38 cm)

Muslin

- Bag muslin base: 14¾ x 15 in (37 x 38 cm)

Lining fabric

- Bag lining: 11¼ x 11½ in (28.4 x 29.4 cm)

Construction Steps

1. Make 84 apple cores as shown in the guide on page 66. Sew the apple cores together to create the bag top, following the layout shown in the diagram on page 132.

2. Layer the bag top, batting, and muslin base. Mark the finishing lines and quilt as shown in the diagram on page 132.

3. Staystitch ¹⁄₁₆ in (2 mm) outside the finishing lines. Trim into shape, leaving ¼ in (7 mm) seam allowance.

4. Fold the bag in half with right sides together. Sew together along the sides.

5. Miter the corners: Press the side seams open. Align each side seam with the bottom fold. Sew across the corners with a 3 ⅛ in (8 cm) seam. Trim the excess fabric, leaving ¼ in (7 mm) seam allowance.

6. Make the yoyo flowers as shown in the diagram below. Sew them to the bag front.

7. Make the lining: Fold the lining in half with right sides together. Sew together along the sides. Repeat step 5 to miter the corners. Insert the lining into the bag with wrong sides together. Baste together around the bag opening.

8. Align the wrong side of the handles with the lining so the handles are facing down (refer to the diagram on page 132 for handle placement). Sew the handles in place, taking care to stitch in the bag opening seam allowance. This will ensure that the raw edges of the handles are covered once the binding is attached.

9. Bind the opening (refer to page 92): With right sides together, sew the short ends of the chenille trim to form a loop matching the size of the opening. With right sides together, sew the chenille trim to the bag. Wrap the chenille trim around the seam allowances and hand stitch to the lining.

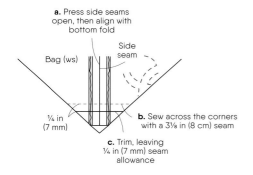

a. Press side seams open, then align with bottom fold

Side seam

Bag (ws)

¼ in (7 mm)

b. Sew across the corners with a 3⅛ in (8 cm) seam

c. Trim, leaving ¼ in (7 mm) seam allowance

Finished Diagram

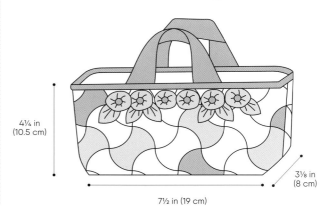

4¼ in (10.5 cm)

3⅛ in (8 cm)

7½ in (19 cm)

HOW TO MAKE THE YOYO FLOWERS

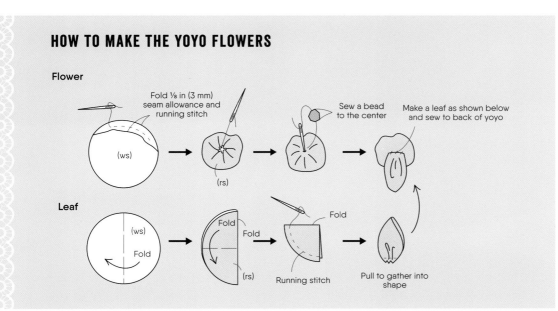

Flower

(ws)

Fold ⅛ in (3 mm) seam allowance and running stitch

(rs)

Sew a bead to the center

Make a leaf as shown below and sew to back of yoyo

Leaf

(ws)

Fold

Fold

Fold

Fold

(rs)

Running stitch

Pull to gather into shape

FLOWER PATCH MINI QUILT

Shown on page 34

Materials

- **Fabric A:** One fat quarter
- **Fabric B:** One fat quarter
- **Appliqué fabric:** Assorted print scraps
- **Border/binding fabric:** ¾ yd (0.7 m)
- **Backing fabric:** ¾ yd (0.7 m)
- **Batting:** 21 in (53 cm) square

- 1¾ yds (1.6 m) of ¾ in (1.7 cm) wide lace
- No. 25 embroidery floss in green

• Sew using ¼ in (7 mm) seam allowance, unless otherwise noted.

• Stitch in the ditch around all appliqué and patchwork pieces.

Project Diagram

Diagrams show finished measurements (seam allowance not included).

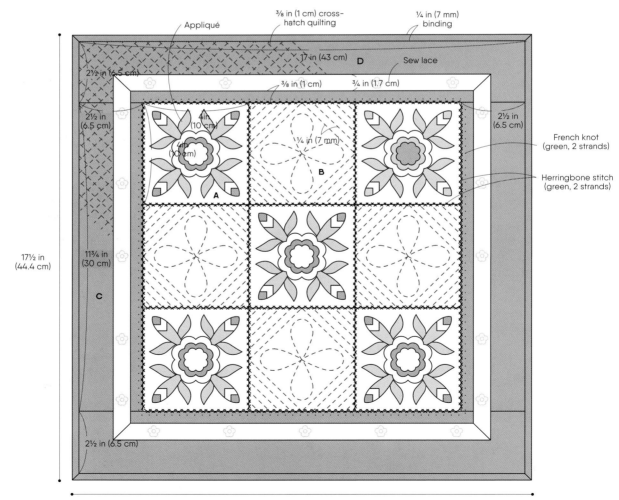

Cutting Instructions

Trace and cut out the templates on Pattern Sheet B. Cut out the following fabric pieces, adding ⅛ in (3 mm) seam allowance.

Appliqué fabric

- Appliqué motif pieces

Cut out the following fabric pieces, which do not have templates, according to the measurements below (these measurements include seam allowance).

Fabric A

- A (cut 5): 4½ in (11.4 cm) squares

Fabric B

- B (cut 4): 4½ in (11.4 cm) squares

Border/binding fabric

- C borders (cut 2): 3 x 12¼ in (7.9 x 31.4 cm)
- D borders (cut 2): 3 x 17½ in (7.9 x 44.4 cm)
- Binding: 2¼ yds (2.1 m) of 1¼ in (3 cm) wide single-fold bias binding

Batting

- Quilt batting: 21 in (53 cm) square

Backing fabric

- Quilt backing: 21 in (53 cm) square

Construction Steps

1. Appliqué the motifs onto the five A squares as shown in the guide on page 68.

Appliqué

2. Alternately sew A and B squares together into three rows of three. Sew the rows together to create the quilt top as shown in the diagram on page 134.

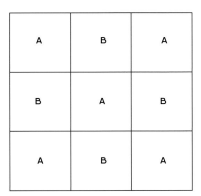

A	B	A
B	A	B
A	B	A

3. Sew the C borders to the left and right edges of the quilt.

4. Sew the D borders to the top and bottom edges of the quilt.

5. Sew the lace to the borders, following the placement noted in the diagram on page 134.

6. Layer the quilt top, batting and backing. Quilt as shown in the diagram on page 134. **Note:** There is a quilting template on Pattern Sheet B. Trim the excess batting and backing to match the size of the quilt top.

7. Embroider as shown in the diagram on page 134.

Herringbone Stitch

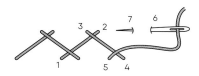

French Knot

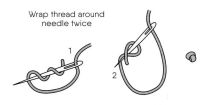

Wrap thread around needle twice

8. Bind the quilt (refer to page 45).

BOXY BRODERIE TOTE

Shown on page 35

Materials

- **Front/back fabric:** One fat eighth of striped fabric
- **Appliqué fabric:** Scraps of large scale floral print
- **Bottom/binding fabric:** On fat quarter of solid beige linen
- **Gusset fabric:** One fat eighth of brown print
- **Lining fabric:** ¾ yd (0.7 m)

- **Batting:** 23¾ x 26¾ in (60 x 68 cm)
- 1 yd (1 m) of rickrack
- One set of 12 in (30 cm) handles
- No. 25 embroidery floss in beige

Sew using ¼ in (7 mm) seam allowance, unless otherwise noted.

Project Diagram

Diagrams show finished measurements (seam allowance not included).

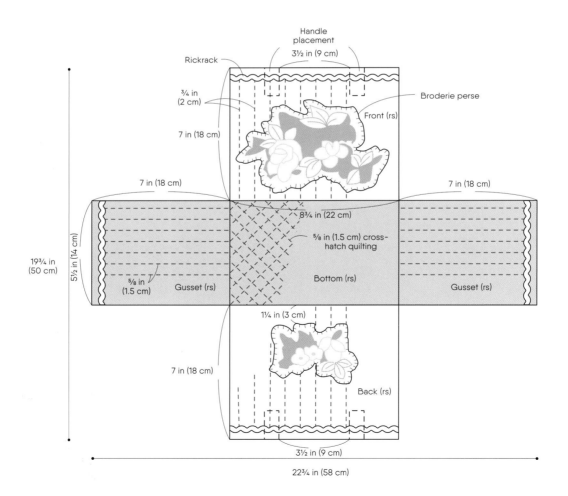

Cutting Instructions

For the broderie perse, cut out two motifs from the appliqué fabric following the instructions on page 74. Cut out the following fabric pieces, which do not have templates, according to the measurements below (these measurements include seam allowance).

Front/back fabric
- Front: 7½ x 9¼ in (19.4 x 23.4 cm)
- Back: 7½ x 9¼ in (19.4 x 23.4 cm)

Bottom/binding fabric:
- Bottom: 6 x 9¼ in (15.4 x 23.4 cm)
- Binding: 2½ yds (2.3 m) of 1¼ in (3 cm) wide single-fold bias binding

Gusset fabric
- Gussets (cut 2): 6 x 7½ in (15.4 x 19.4 cm)

Batting
- Bag batting: Cut out in the shape of the assembled bag top after completing step 3, but make it a couple inches larger on each side

Lining fabric
- Bag lining: Cut out in the shape of the assembled bag top after completing step 3, but make it a couple inches larger on each side

Construction Steps

1. Appliqué the motifs onto the front and back pieces using the broderie perse technique shown in the guide on page 75 (refer to the diagram on page 136 for placement).

2. With right sides together, sew the front and back pieces to the long edges of the bottom. Take care to position the back upside down so that the motif will appear right side up once the bag is folded into place.

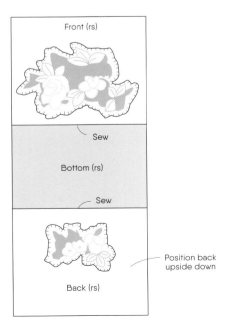

3. With right sides together, sew a gusset piece to each short edge of the bottom.

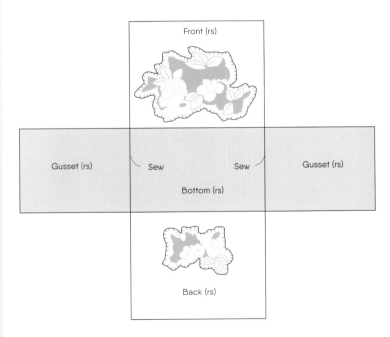

4. Layer the assembled bag top, batting, and lining. Quilt as shown in the diagram on page 136. Trim the excess batting and lining to match the size of the bag top.

5. Hand stitch the rickrack to the bag top as shown in the diagram on page 136.

6. Bind the edges: With right sides together, sew the binding to the bag top, mitering the corners (refer to page 45). Sew the short ends of the binding together and press the seam allowance open. Wrap the binding around the seam allowance and hand stitch to the lining.

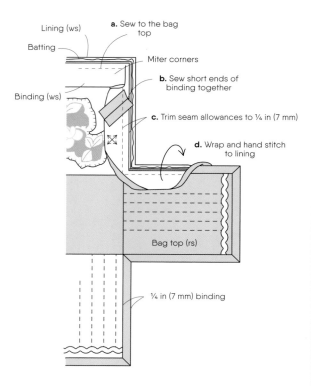

Lining (ws)

Batting

Binding (ws)

a. Sew to the bag top

Miter corners

b. Sew short ends of binding together

c. Trim seam allowances to ¼ in (7 mm)

d. Wrap and hand stitch to lining

Bag top (rs)

¼ in (7 mm) binding

7. Fold the bag into a box shape by aligning the gussets with the front and back. Working from the outside of the bag, sew the front and back to the gussets, just outside of the binding seam.

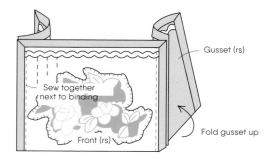

Gusset (rs)

Sew together next to binding

Fold gusset up

Front (rs)

8. Use the embroidery floss to sew the handles to the bag outside, following the placement noted in the diagram on page 136.

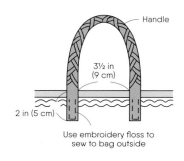

Handle

3½ in (9 cm)

2 in (5 cm)

Use embroidery floss to sew to bag outside

Finished Diagram

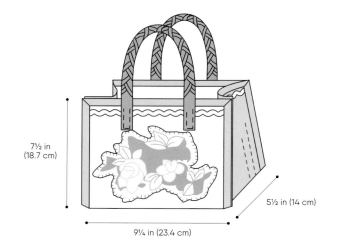

7½ in (18.7 cm)

5½ in (14 cm)

9¼ in (23.4 cm)

FLORAL LACE BASKET BAG

Shown on page 36

Materials

- **Bag fabric:** ½ yd (0.5 m) of lace print fabric
- **Appliqué fabric:** Scraps of a large scale floral print
- **Bottom/binding fabric:** ¾ yd (0.7 m) of solid black
- **Lining fabric:** ¾ yd (0.7 m)
- ¾ yd (0.7 m) of muslin
- **Batting:** 23¾ x 43½ in (60 x 110 cm)

- **Fusible interfacing:** 19¾ x 39½ in (50 x 100 cm)
- **Plastic sheeting:** 6 x 14¼ in (15 x 36 cm)
- One set of 13½ in (34 cm) handles

Sew using ¼ in (7 mm) seam allowance, unless otherwise noted.

Project Diagram

Diagrams show finished measurements (seam allowance not included).

Bag Outside

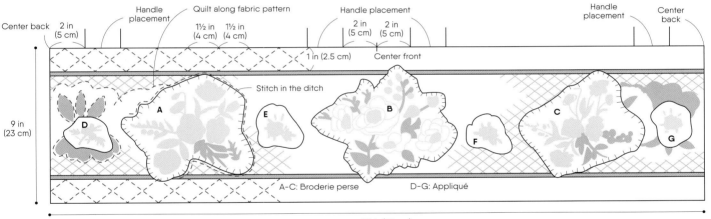

Bottom

Bottom Plate

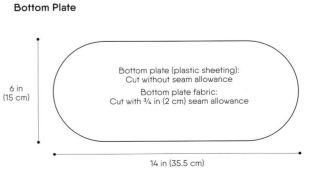

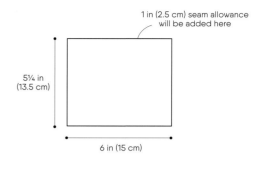

Lining

Center back

2¾ in (7 cm)

9 in
(23 cm)

Center front fold

Inside pocket
placement

37 in (94 cm)

Inside Pocket

1 in (2.5 cm) seam allowance
will be added here

5¼ in
(13.5 cm)

6 in (15 cm)

Cutting Instructions

For the broderie perse, cut out three large motifs from the appliqué fabric following the instructions on page 74. For the traditional appliqué, use the same process to cut three small motifs from the appliqué fabric. Trace and cut out the templates on Pattern Sheet B. Cut out the following fabric pieces a few inches larger than the template on each side. These pieces will be trimmed into shape once the layers have been quilted:

Bottom/binding fabric

• 1 bottom

Batting

• 1 bottom

Muslin

• 1 bottom muslin base

Cut out the following fabric pieces, adding ¼ in (7 mm) seam allowance.

Fusible interfacing

• 1 bottom

Lining fabric

• 1 bottom

Cut out the following fabric piece, adding ¾ in (2 cm) seam allowance.

Muslin

• 1 bottom plate fabric

Do not add seam allowance when cutting out the following piece:

Plastic sheeting

• 1 bottom plate

Cut out the following fabric pieces, which do not have templates, according to the measurements below (these measurements include seam allowance).

Bag fabric

• Bag outside: 13 x 41 in (33 x 104 cm)

Batting

• Bag batting: 13 x 41 in (33 x 104 cm)

Muslin

• Bag muslin base: 13 x 41 in (33 x 104 cm)

Fusible interfacing

• Bag interfacing: 9½ x 37½ in (24.4 x 95.4 cm)

Lining fabric

• Bag lining: 9½ x 37½ in (24.4 x 95.4 cm)
• Inside pocket: 6⅝ x 6¾ in (17 x 17 cm)

Bottom/binding fabric

• Binding: 1¼ yds (1.2 m) of 1¼ in (3 cm) wide single-fold bias binding

Construction Steps

1. Mark the quilting and finishing lines on the bag outside and bottom (refer to the diagrams on page 139). **Note:** It will be difficult to mark the lines on the bag outside once the motifs have been appliquéd in place.

2. Appliqué motifs A–C onto the bag outside using the broderie perse technique shown in the guide on page 75. Fold the raw edges under and appliqué motifs D–G onto the bag outside using the traditional appliqué technique shown in the guide on page 69.

3. Layer the bag outside, batting, and muslin base. Quilt as shown below and in the diagram on page 139.

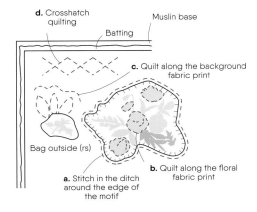

d. Crosshatch quilting
Muslin base
Batting
c. Quilt along the background fabric print
Bag outside (rs)
b. Quilt along the floral fabric print
a. Stitch in the ditch around the edge of the motif

4. Trim into shape, leaving ¼ in (7 mm) seam allowance. Adhere fusible interfacing to the wrong side of the muslin base.

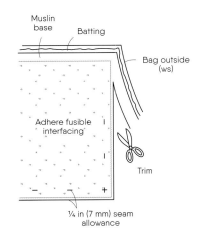

Muslin base
Batting
Bag outside (ws)
Adhere fusible interfacing
Trim
¼ in (7 mm) seam allowance

Note: This bag is constructed with batting, a muslin base, and a layer of fusible interfacing to provide support and structure. A separate lining will be added to hide these layers. You could also use a foam interfacing instead and skip these steps.

5. Layer the bottom, batting, and muslin base. Quilt as shown in the diagram on page 139. Trim into shape, leaving ¼ in (7 mm) seam allowance. Adhere fusible interfacing to the wrong side of the muslin base.

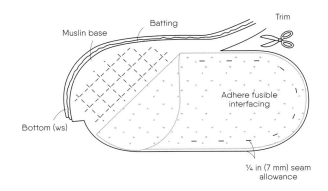

Muslin base
Batting
Trim
Bottom (ws)
Adhere fusible interfacing
¼ in (7 mm) seam allowance

6. Fold the bag outside in half with right sides together and sew. With right sides together, sew the bottom to the bag outside, leaving ⅜ in (1 cm) opening at the seam for the cord ends.

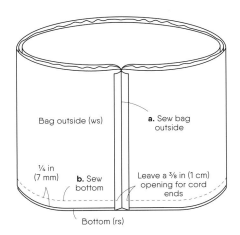

Bag outside (ws)
a. Sew bag outside
¼ in (7 mm)
b. Sew bottom
Leave a ⅜ in (1 cm) opening for cord ends
Bottom (rs)

7. Turn the bag right side out. Hand stitch the cord to the bottom seam. Insert the cord ends into the opening

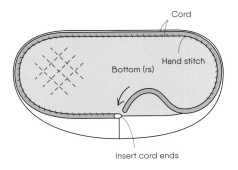

Cord
Hand stitch
Bottom (rs)
Insert cord ends

8. Sew the opening closed, stitching through the cords. Trim the excess cord.

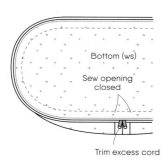

Bottom (ws)

Sew opening closed

Trim excess cord

9. Make the bottom plate as shown below, then hand stitch it in place on the inside of the bag.

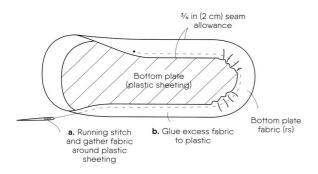

¾ in (2 cm) seam allowance

Bottom plate (plastic sheeting)

Bottom plate fabric (rs)

a. Running stitch and gather fabric around plastic sheeting

b. Glue excess fabric to plastic

10. Make the inside pocket (refer to page 92): Fold and press the top edge of the inside pocket over ⅜ in (1 cm) to the wrong side. Fold and press the top edge over another ⅝ in (1.5 cm). Fold and press the remaining three edges over ⅜ in (1 cm) to the wrong side. Topstitch the pocket to the bag lining, following the placement noted in the diagram on page 140.

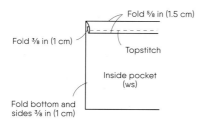

Fold ⅝ in (1.5 cm)

Fold ⅜ in (1 cm)

Topstitch

Inside pocket (ws)

Fold bottom and sides ⅜ in (1 cm)

11. Make the lining: Fold the bag lining in half with right sides together and sew. With right sides together, sew the bottom lining to the bag lining. Insert the lining into the bag outside with wrong sides together. Baste together around the bag opening.

12. Align the wrong side of the handles with the lining so the handles are facing down (refer to the diagram on page 139 for handle placement). Sew the handles in place, taking care to stitch in the bag opening seam allowance. This will ensure that the raw edges of the handles are covered once the binding is attached.

13. Bind the opening: With right sides together, sew the short ends of the binding to form a loop matching the size of the opening. With right sides together, sew the binding to the bag. Wrap the binding around the seam allowances and hand stitch to the lining.

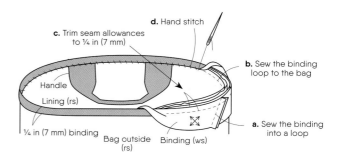

c. Trim seam allowances to ¼ in (7 mm)

d. Hand stitch

b. Sew the binding loop to the bag

Handle

Lining (rs)

¼ in (7 mm) binding

Bag outside (rs)

Binding (ws)

a. Sew the binding into a loop

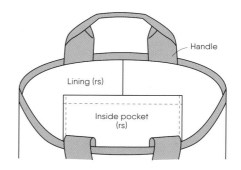

Handle

Lining (rs)

Inside pocket (rs)

Finished Diagram

9¼ in (23.7 cm)

6¼ in (16 cm)

15 in (38 cm)